T2-CAP-364

Ballistics

Other titles in the Crime Scene Investigations series:

Ballistics

by Andrew A. Kling

LUCENT BOOKS
A part of Gale, Cengage Learning

GALE
CENGAGE Learning

Detroit • New York • San Francisco • New Haven, Conn • Waterville, Maine • London

GALE
CENGAGE Learning™

LIBRARY OF CONGRESS CATALOGING-IN-PUBLICATION DATA

Kling, Andrew A., 1961-
    Ballistics / by Andrew A. Kling.
        p. cm. — (Crime scene investigations)
    Includes bibliographical references and index.
    ISBN 978-1-59018-988-7 (hardcover)
    1. Forensic ballistics — Juvenile literature. 2. Ballistics — Juvenile literature.
    3. Forensic sciences — Juvenile literature. 4. Criminal investigation — Juvenile
    literature. I. Title.
        HV8077.K55 2009
        363.25'62—dc22
                                                                         2008039974

Lucent Books
27500 Drake Rd
Farmington Hills MI 48331

ISBN-13: 978-1-59018-988-7
ISBN-10: 1-59018-988-4

Printed in the United States of America
2 3 4 5 6 7 12 11 10 09

Contents

Foreword

The popularity of crime scene and investigative crime shows on television has come as a surprise to many who work in the field. The main surprise is the concept that crime scene analysts are the true crime solvers, when in truth, it takes dozens of people, doing many different jobs, to solve a crime. Often, the crime scene analyst's contribution is a small one. One Minnesota forensic scientist says that the public "has gotten the wrong idea. Because I work in a lab similar to the ones on *CSI*, people seem to think I'm solving crimes left and right—just me and my microscope. They don't believe me when I tell them that it's just the investigators that are solving crimes, not me."

Crime scene analysts do have an important role to play, however. Science has rapidly added a whole new dimension to gathering and assessing evidence. Modern crime labs can match a hair of a murder suspect to one found on a murder victim, for example, or recover a latent fingerprint from a threatening letter, or use a powerful microscope to match tool marks made during the wiring of an explosive device to a tool in a suspect's possession.

Probably the most exciting of the forensic scientist's tools is DNA analysis. DNA can be found in just one drop of blood, a dribble of saliva on a toothbrush, or even the residue from a fingerprint. Some DNA analysis techniques enable scientists to tell with certainty, for example, whether a drop of blood on a suspect's shirt is that of a murder victim.

While these exciting techniques are now an essential part of many investigations, they cannot solve crimes alone. "DNA doesn't come with a name and address on it," says the Minnesota forensic scientist. "It's great if you have someone in custody to match the sample to, but otherwise, it doesn't help.

That's the investigator's job. We can have all the great DNA evidence in the world, and without a suspect, it will just sit on a shelf. We've all seen cases with very little forensic evidence get solved by the resourcefulness of a detective."

While forensic specialists get the most media attention today, the work of detectives still forms the core of most criminal investigations. Their job, in many ways, has changed little over the years. Most cases are still solved through the persistence and determination of a criminal detective whose work may be anything but glamorous. Many cases require routine, even mind-numbing tasks. After the July 2005 bombings in London, for example, police officers sat in front of video players watching thousands of hours of closed-circuit television tape from security cameras throughout the city, and as a result were able to get the first images of the bombers.

The Lucent Books Crime Scene Investigations series explores the variety of ways crimes are solved. Titles cover particular crimes such as murder, specific cases such as the killing of three civil rights workers in Mississippi, or the role specialists such as medical examiners play in solving crimes. Each title in the series demonstrates the ways a crime may be solved, from the various applications of forensic science and technology to the reasoning of investigators. Sidebars examine both the limits and possibilities of the new technologies and present crime statistics, career information, and step-by-step explanations of scientific and legal processes.

The Crime Scene Investigations series strives to be both informative and realistic about how members of law enforcement—criminal investigators, forensic scientists, and others—solve crimes, for it is essential that student researchers understand that crime solving is rarely quick or easy. Many factors—from a detective's dogged pursuit of one tenuous lead to a suspect's careless mistakes to sheer luck to complex calculations computed in the lab—are all part of crime solving today.

The "D.C. Snipers"

On the evening of October 2, 2002, a single bullet sped down the barrel of a Bushmaster XM-15 semiautomatic .223 caliber rifle. The small piece of metal exploded from the rifle's muzzle at a speed of 3,200 feet per second (975 meters per second), or nearly three times the speed of sound. It headed toward its target, a man walking across the parking lot of a Shoppers Food Warehouse in Wheaton, Maryland.

The bullet slammed into James D. Martin, a fifty-five-year-old computer analyst who had stopped for groceries, with more than 1,200 foot-pounds of force, severing his spinal cord and perforating his aorta. Witnesses at the scene called 911, but Martin died from massive blood loss before paramedics could reach him.

From the trunk of dark blue 1990 Chevrolet Caprice, the man who had fired the Bushmaster watched the scene unfold through a small hole. A second man, the car's driver, also surveyed the chaos they had created before slowly driving away. Over the next three weeks, similar scenes occurred in the communities surrounding Washington, D.C. The nation and the world watched in horror over each shooting and in anticipation of the capture of the individual or individuals responsible, who came to be known by such names as the "Beltway Sniper" and the "D.C. Snipers."

Victims in the Wrong Place at the Wrong Time

On October 3, the day after James Martin's shooting, five more people, three men and two women, were each killed by a single gunshot. Early that morning, James Buchanan was shot while mowing the lawn in front of an auto dealership. Less than an hour later, at 8:12 A.M., Premkumar Walekar, a taxi driver, stopped to fill his tank. A loud crack filled the air and Walekar staggered for help before collapsing near the pumps. A devoted father, Walekar always encouraged his daughter, Andrea, to do well in school and finish college, an opportunity that he had to pass up. The sniper's bullet shattered his dream of watching Andrea graduate.

At 8:37, Sarah Ramos, a housekeeper and babysitter, sat down to read on a bus stop bench. Suddenly, Sarah slumped over, her book dropping to the ground. At her funeral a few days later, a close friend described Sarah: "Besides walking in with a smile, she walked in the room with something that filled your soul with love. She represented the very foundation of love of family."[1]

Less than two hours later, a single bullet took the life of Lori Ann Lewis-Rivera, a twenty-five-year-old babysitter, as she vacuumed her car. The snipers' sixth victim was an elderly man, Pascal Charlot, who was out for an evening walk when he was shot at 9:15 P.M.

The Clues Emerge

By this time, area and federal law enforcement investigators knew they had a serial killer who seemed to choose his targets at random. One of the challenges they faced was that each victim of the attacks was different. Officials were at a loss to try to connect the victims to any common factor. Age, ethnicity, profession, gender, or race did not tie any of them together. The only thing the victims seemed to have in common was simply that they had been targeted.

As the days stretched into weeks, the numbers grew. On October 4, Caroline Seawell, a stay-at-home mother who was loading Halloween decorations into her minivan, became the seventh victim. However, this time, the shot was not as precise as earlier ones. This bullet tore through her abdomen; though critically wounded, she survived the attack. The next victim, the snipers' youngest, survived as well.

Police stand outside of Benjamin Tasker Middle School after the shooting of 13-year-old Iran Brown on October 7, 2002.

The Youngest Victim

Three days later, on October 7 at 8:09 A.M., Tanya Brown dropped off her thirteen-year-old nephew, Iran Brown, at his local middle school. Though both were concerned about the killings of the previous week, neither considered that a child would become a victim. As the boy approached the brick building, a man in the trunk of an old blue car peered through a rifle's electronic sights and squeezed the trigger. Less than a second later, Iran fell to the ground, shot in the abdomen.

Luckily, his aunt Tanya was a nurse. Without hesitation, she grabbed Iran, put him back into her car, and drove as fast as she dared to the nearest clinic. The bullet had wreaked extensive damage to Iran's stomach, pancreas, spleen, and one of his lungs, but Iran would live.

The Final Victims

On the night of October 9, Dean Harold Meyers, a Vietnam War veteran who loved hot rods and Corvettes, stopped at a gas station to fill up his tank after working late. Two days later, Kenneth Bridges stopped off at a different gas station. He was on his way home to Philadelphia. Both men died of injuries caused by a single rifle bullet.

The snipers struck again on the evening of October 14. This time, Linda Franklin and her husband had finished shopping at a Home Depot store and were loading their purchases into the trunk of their car. Linda was an FBI analyst who worked in the bureau's Cyber-Crimes Division and was not involved in investigations of the area shootings. However, that changed as she came into the view of the Bushmaster's holographic sights. Linda became the eleventh person to be shot and the ninth to die. Yet, the shootings continued.

On October 19, Stephanie and Jeff Hopper were walking to their car after finishing dinner at a Ponderosa Steakhouse, when a bullet struck Jeff in the abdomen. The high-powered rifle's bullet severely damaged his stomach but he survived. Unfortunately, the next victim, Conrad Johnson, would not survive. Johnson, a husband and father of two boys, loved being a bus driver. On October 22, Conrad was shot in the stomach

Police officers surround the car driven by Washington, D.C., sniper suspects John Allen Muhammad and Lee Boyd Malvo.

while standing on the steps of his bus. A man with a ready smile and a kind word, Johnson proved to be the snipers' last victim, because on October 24, 2002, John Allen Muhammad and Lee Boyd Malvo were arrested and charged with murder. The "D.C. Snipers" had been caught.

Examining the Evidence

Throughout Muhammad and Malvo's three-week killing spree, authorities searched for clues that would link the shootings together and that would lead them to the murderers. At first there seemed to be nothing that tied the events together. However, each shooting left behind a vital clue: the bullets.

Investigators examining the bullet pieces taken from the victims, and the wounds left by the bullets, determined that the shooter was using a high-powered rifle that could be fired from long distances. At first, investigators believed only one person was the sniper; it would be weeks before they learned that there were two snipers. However, the shooting of Iran Brown proved to be the first real break in the case.

Clues left behind at each sniper crime scene helped link all of the cases together. For example, by studying bullet casings at each scene, one of which is shown here, it was determined that the bullets all came from the same weapon.

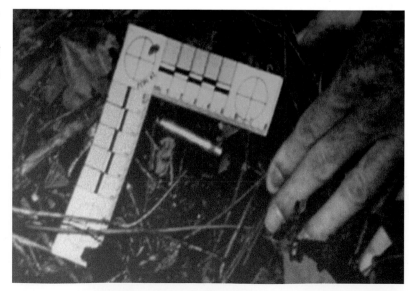

Crime scene investigators found an empty .223 caliber "casing," or lower part of a cartridge, near Iran's school that was the same size as the bullets that had killed or wounded the other victims. Along with evidence gathered from the previous victims and crime scenes, firearms examiners now had bullets, wound patterns, and a shell casing.

While firearms examiners investigated the ammunition, trained medical personnel examined the victims. Bodies of murder victims must be examined by a medical examiner, a doctor who is trained to look for criminal evidence. This includes bullet fragments, the patterns of wounds caused by a bullet's impact and its penetration into a body, and the type of internal damage done by the bullet. Medical examiners found that the bullets extracted from the victims' bodies were the same size. That told the police the bullets were fired from a rifle. When investigators found shell casings near Iran Brown's middle school and later at the Ponderosa restaurant parking lot, ballistics experts could identify them as having been fired from the same rifle.

Further information led the crime scene investigators to an additional important discovery. Analyses of the shootings enabled them to determine the angle of the shots. It appeared that the rifle was fired from a position only a few feet above the ground. Investigators at first thought that the shooter was either kneeling or crouching. The police did not yet know that the sniper fired from the trunk of a car. Only later would they learn about the old blue Caprice.

Finally, October 24, 2002, when Muhammad and Malvo were arrested, a Bushmaster XM-15 rifle with electronic scope was found in the trunk of their car. "We have the weapon. It is off the street,"[2] said Charles Moose, police chief of Montgomery County, Maryland, where many of the killings took place. The people of Washington, D.C., and its neighbors breathed a collective sigh of relief. Law enforcement agencies did as well. However, for the forensic scientists, much of their work lay ahead.

The Damage Left Behind

Charles Moose, chief of Maryland's Montgomery County Police Department, led the department that headed the investigation of the D.C.-area shootings. He watched as the snipers' bullets tore apart the lives of his community.

The three-week sniper siege left a permanent mark on Montgomery County and the Washington, D.C., area. The snipers' bullets did permanent damage. They left ten people dead. They seriously wounded three others. The snipers' marksmanship shot holes in the lives of the families of these victims. Some of that damage can never be repaired. The people who died will be missed, forever, by their loved ones. Some of the people who lived through the siege will be frightened, forever, by what happened to them. The sniper shootings will be the defining moment in the childhoods of the little boys and girls who had to go to school terrified that some unknown person was going to shoot them down on the playground.

The shootings left a mark on me, too.... No matter where I go with the rest of my life, and no matter what else I do, I will always be the police chief who led the sniper task force.

Quoted in Charles A. Moose and Charles Fleming, *Three Weeks in October: The Manhunt for the Serial Sniper.* New York: Dutton, 2003, pp. 309–10.

Forensic Ballistics and the "D.C. Snipers"

"Forensic ballistics" (also known as "firearms identification") is the science of studying the usage of firearms and ammunition in shooting incidents, and it played an enormous role in the story of the "D.C. Snipers." Firearms examiners were certain that the Bushmaster had been used in all but three of the shootings. The cartridge casings found at the middle school and restaurant also matched ammunition test-fired from the Bushmaster. Finally, fingerprints on the rifle matched Malvo's prints. The chain of evidence had caught the men in an inescapable net, and these analyses became a central piece of evidence in their murder trials.

Muhammad's trial began in October 2003 and Malvo's trial began a month later. Both men were convicted of murder. Malvo received ninety years without parole. Muhammad was sentenced to death by lethal injection. At the time of this writing, both were still in prison in Virginia.

Forensic ballistics helped put the "D.C. Snipers" behind bars and demonstrated that it is an integral part of law enforcement. Soldiers, scientists, inventors, and doctors have studied the effects of firearms and of ammunition since the 1600s. Yet forensic ballistics is a relatively new science, only gaining widespread acceptance since the 1920s. Today, a well-staffed crime lab provides detectives, police officers, and forensic examiners with the tools to conduct a thorough criminal investigation whenever firearms are involved.

CHAPTER 1

Firearms and Bullets

Forensic ballistics is the scientific study of firearms, bullets, and bullet behavior after being fired from a gun.

For law enforcement personnel, a callout to a crime scene may begin a long and complex series of interlocking investigations into the nature, cause, and persons responsible for the incident. Specialists known as crime scene investigators assist law enforcement officers and detectives to uncover the clues at the scene. Because the United States has more firearms, and more firearms violence, than any other country, these clues often involve evidence left behind by firearms.

Firearms have been used for hundreds of years. The world's oldest gun was found by archeologists in China. They believe it was dropped on a battlefield in Manchuria in 1288. By the 1600s,

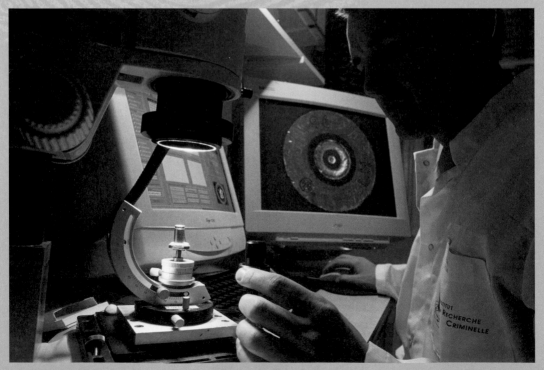

A New Word for a New Technology

In the early days of firearms development, each piece was handmade. The size of the barrel created by the gunsmith was often based on personal preference, and the ammunition was created to fit that individual gun. Faced with the need to be able to define the size of the gun's barrel and the ammunition that would fit inside it, gunsmiths began using the word "caliber" to express the gun's capacity.

Derived from an old Arabic word for a form used by a shoemaker to create footwear, caliber today refers to the interior diameter of a gun's barrel, and is expressed in hundreds of an inch. Therefore, a gun that is a ".32 caliber" has a barrel diameter of 32/100ths of an inch. The ammunition that fits a .32 caliber gun, consequently, has an outer diameter of 32/100ths of an inch also.

As the metric system became the international standard for measurement, caliber measurements were also affected, and have often been converted to millimeters. For example, a rifle or pistol that was once called a .30 caliber may now carry the designation of 7.62 mm.

firearms were becoming essential equipment for the armies of European nations, and helped pave the way for conquerors who spread out across the globe to the Americas, Africa, Asia, and Australia. By the 1900s, millions of firearms, and the ammunition for them, were being mass produced.

During this time, the science of forensic ballistics was developed to keep pace with the expanding number of crimes committed using firearms. This science examines firearms, bullets, and bullet behavior after being fired from a gun, and provides a quantitative, or measurable, way to compare crime scene evidence from multiple cases. The foundation of this science is an understanding of the construction of ammunition and the mechanics of firearms.

Inside Ammunition

In everyday language, people sometimes use the word "bullet" to refer to the ammunition that is loaded into or fired from a weapon. However, to a crime scene investigator, and particularly to a specialist in forensic ballistics, a bullet is only part of the ammunition. In fact, the ammunition is made of several parts; an outer casing contains the bullet gunpowder and primer. The gunpowder serves as a propellant when it ignites, and the primer ignites the powder. For a scientist, the more accurate term for this assemblage is "cartridge" or "round."

Bullet casings differ greatly. Pictured here are nine different types of casings.

Investigators can determine a great deal about the firearm involved in a shooting from the bullets. Bullets fall into several broad categories. Those constructed of lead are soft; they can easily change shape and break up into fragments when they strike a target. Consequently, a lead bullet fragment found at a crime scene can help investigators focus on a particular type of

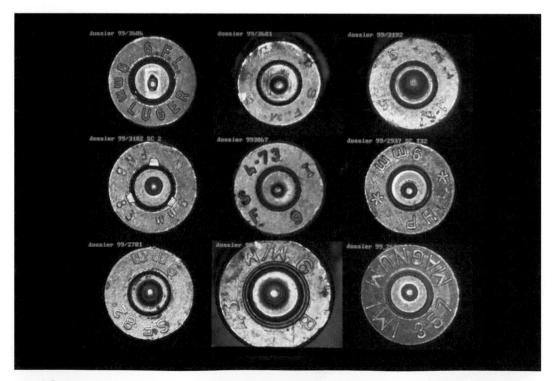

weapon. Lead alloy bullets are harder, and are made by combining lead with tin or antimony. They do not change their shape or break apart as easily. Consequently, an intact bullet—one that seems to be intact and without fragments missing—can lead investigators towards certain makes of ammunition that use lead-alloy bullets.

Investigators may find other types of bullets at a crime scene. Some bullets are constructed of a lead core with a full or partial "jacket," or outer covering, made of steel, copper, or a mixture of copper and nickel. "Semi-jacketed" bullets are partially coated with, or plated by, a thin metal layer that leaves the lead core partially uncovered. A lead core that is completely covered by a metal layer is encased by a "full metal jacket." Investigators know that these designs are only used in certain weapons, and so they provide vital evidence about what may have occurred at the scene.

Regardless of their construction, all types of cartridges and bullets act very much the same way. In historic firearms, a complicated and time-consuming series of actions were required before the round was fired. Today, firing a round consists mostly of simply placing a cartridge inside the firing chamber in front of the firing pin, either mechanically or by hand, and pulling a trigger.

A Pull of the Trigger

For a crime scene investigator, the pull of a trigger sets into motion two important series of actions. The first series of actions happen almost simultaneously. When the trigger is pulled, the firing pin hits a cylinder of primer of gunpowder (or another chemical mixture, such as potassium perchlorate) in the base of the cartridge. The burning primer ignites the gunpowder, and the explosion releases gases inside the cartridge.

> ## By the Numbers
>
> # 3,700,000
>
> **Approximate number of firearms manufactured in the United States in 2006, according to statistics released by the Bureau of Alcohol, Tobacco, Firearms, and Explosives.**

When the trigger of a loaded firearm is squeezed, a bullet is forced out of the barrel at a great speed nearly instantaneously.

As the gases expand, the bullet is forced down and out of the barrel at a tremendous speed. The shell casing, the part of the cartridge left after the powder explodes and the bullet is propelled outward, slams against the back wall of the firing chamber. Finally, the spent casing is removed from the firing chamber, either manually or by a mechanism called an ejector. Depending on the type of firearm, another mechanism called an extractor then grabs the next cartridge and seats it in the firing chamber.

The second series of actions take place over a longer period of time. These are the actions associated with the investigation of the shooting. The pull of the trigger may create a wealth of information about the firearm and the individual involved. The shooter may have left fingerprints on the trigger, the firearm, and the cartridges. Additionally, other scientific information results from the pull of a trigger. The spent cartridges and fired bullets allow investigators to formulate preliminary theories at the scene.

One of the first theories they make concerns the type of weapon involved. Firearms are classified into three broad categories: handguns, rifles, and shotguns. Handguns, as their name implies, are held in the shooter's hand. Rifles and shotguns are designed to be braced against the shooter's shoulder. While all three are used in crimes, handguns are the most prevalent.

The Challenge of Handguns

Handguns are manufactured in a wide variety of designs by numerous companies around the world. In addition, individuals craft replicas of historic models or restore antiques to working condition. The challenge for forensic ballistics examiners is to not only understand how older or historic handguns behaved, but also to stay up-to-date with advances in handgun technology.

Handguns, also called pistols, include revolvers, semiautomatic pistols, and machine pistols. Historically, single-shot pistols were followed by the invention of the revolver; by the time the United States had expanded to the west in the mid- to late 1800s, the revolver was a popular choice for outlaws and lawmen alike. These vintage "six shooters" carried six cartridges. Today, some revolvers still carry six cartridges; others carry only five. Revolvers are named after the rotating cylinder that holds the gun's cartridges. With each pull of the trigger, the firing pin hits the cartridge, and a bullet flies down the barrel. Then, the cylinder rotates and places the next cartridge in front of the firing pin. After the bullet is fired, the cartridge's casing is left behind in the cylinder and has to be removed by hand before new cartridges are loaded.

A magazine, which holds a number of bullet cartridges, is loaded into a semiautomatic handgun.

If the revolver was the favorite handgun of the "Wild West," the semiautomatic pistol might be seen as its modern counterpart. In a semiautomatic handgun, the cartridges are held in a "magazine" that slides into the handle of the pistol. The magazine holds a stack of cartridges. Each time the trigger is pulled, a cartridge is pushed from the magazine into the firing chamber. Unlike a revolver, the casing of the fired cartridge is automatically ejected from the pistol by a mechanism and a new cartridge from the magazine is slid in front of the firing hammer. The energy from the recoil, or backward motion of a fired piston, is used to eject the empty cartridge case, load the next cartridge, and cock the hammer. Since this sequence is automatic, it is easy to fire multiple shots.

In a semiautomatic pistol, the handgun fires one round each time the trigger is pulled, and only one round for each pull of the trigger. A machine pistol works in a similar fashion, but has one significant difference. As in the semiautomatic pistol, a machine pistol's cartridges are also stacked in a clip. When fired, the spent casings are flung from the gun and a new cartridge is slid into the firing chamber. However, unlike a semiautomatic pistol, a machine pistol's repeated firing is completely automatic; it fires continually as long as the trigger is held down.

Each of these types of handguns presents a challenge to law enforcement personnel. For example, each manufacturer of machine pistols crafts the weapon in a particular way. The forensic ballistics expert needs to recognize these differences in order to accurately determine the type of weapon used at the scene. However, handguns are not the only type of weapon that law enforcement personnel may encounter. Evidence at a crime scene may point to the use of a different type of firearm. These weapons consist of a much longer barrel and a different firing capability, and are generally called *long guns*.

Using the Comparison Microscope

Since its debut in the 1920s, the comparison microscope has been an essential tool in firearms investigation. The instrument provides the examiner with an efficient method of comparing a cartridge casing or bullet in evidence with another sample from a known origin. The following steps show one method of comparison.

1. The examiner places the evidence piece on the left-hand stage of the instrument and secures it in place with pressure-sensitive wax adhesive.

2. The known sample is placed on the right-hand stage.

3. Starting at the lowest magnification (usually 10x or lower), the examiner compares the class characteristics of the two samples by looking through the eyepieces.

4. The examiner rotates the stages of the samples in order to optimize the view of the toolmarks, such as breechface striations or ejector marks.

5. The examiner moves the images to the left or right for better viewing.

6. Greater magnification can be used for more in-depth investigation.

A Different Class of Firearm

Long guns differ from handguns in two ways. They have much longer barrels, and they have a stock behind the trigger area. The stock is a roughly triangular piece of wood or metal, often padded, which is designed to be placed against the shoulder. Long guns fall into two general categories: rifles and shotguns.

Both are harder to carry and are more difficult to conceal than handguns. In addition, in the United States, they are more loosely regulated than handguns. They can be bought and sold more easily than handguns, as U.S. federal regulations categorize long guns as being used for collecting or for hunting. For investigators, this means that few records of a particular long gun may exist, such as where it was manufactured or when it was last sold, and to whom.

Rifles take their name from the innovation inside the barrel that enables them to fire larger cartridges with greater accuracy than handguns. In the words of researcher N.E. Genge, "Some time ago, a bright machinist realized that a 'rifled' tube—one with spiral marks inside it—results in a more accurate weapon. The spirals inside the bore (the inside of the barrel) cause the [bullet] to spin, keeping it on a straight course as it leaves the tube."[3] This twisting groove is cut inside the barrel during manufacturing, which gives the bullet this spinning motion. This motion is similar to the way an American football spirals when thrown.

This hunter is using a pump action shotgun.

As with handguns, rifles and shotguns come in a variety of styles and designs, and firearms investigators need to understand each type's behavior and characteristics. Rifles may be manufactured with a single shot capacity, in which each cartridge must be loaded individually. Most of these use "bolt action," whereby the firing chamber is opened and closed using a lever called a bolt, which also contains an ejector for the spent shell casing. Bolt action is most common in large caliber hunting rifles. A "pump action" rifle carries a magazine below the barrel, which is slid forward and back to load and eject the cartridges. The classic western television show *The Rifleman* featured the title character using a "lever action" rifle, in which the cartridges are loaded and ejected from a magazine below the barrel by ratcheting a lever behind the trigger guard.

Military forces around the world also use rifles. Most of these are semiautomatic or fully automatic, and have a detachable magazine holding from five to fifty rounds. In some circumstances, these firearms find their way into civilian hands. But as many of these are manufactured for sale to a government's military, they are better documented than conventional rifles, and law enforcement investigators have a better chance of tracing these weapons to a particular individual.

Shotguns have a similar external appearance to rifles, but are called "smoothbores," because their barrels have no interior rifling. A shotgun shell may contain one large projectile (called a slug), a few pellets of large shot, or many tiny pellets. Shotguns are available in single shot, double barrel, pump action, and semiautomatic models.

The wide variety of handguns and long guns from manufacturers and hobbyists around the world presents the forensic ballistics investigator with an ongoing challenge. But each investigator is following in the footsteps of the original developers of the field.

The Evolution of Forensic Ballistics

The revolution in the science of forensic ballistics came when investigators realized that unique markings on a projectile could be linked to the gun that fired it—and hence to the person who pulled the trigger.

As firearms became lighter and more accurate, and manufactured in greater numbers, they ceased to be only for members of the military. Ordinary people began to use them for hunting and for protection. Unfortunately, firearms also became popular with criminals. By the 1800s, the growth of these weapons among criminals was one of the factors that led to the creation of modern police forces in cities around the world. These professionals began to realize that identifying a bullet or a cartridge case would allow them to discover the gun that fired it. One of the first criminal cases to be solved by this application of forensic ballistics took place in 1835, when the story of a butler did not match up with the evidence.

The Butler Did It

One of the first criminal cases to be solved through the use of firearms identification occurred in Southampton, England, in 1835 by Henry Goddard. Goddard was a member of London's Bow Street Runners, one of the world's first police forces. Goddard's regular beat was London, but he was called in by local authorities in Southampton to assist with a burglary at the home of a Mrs. Maxwell.

At the scene, Goddard was informed that shots had been exchanged between the burglars and Joseph Randall, the family butler. According to David Owen, author of *Hidden Evidence: Forty True Crimes and How Forensic Science Helped Solve Them*, Goddard found the butler's story a bit suspicious.

> In those days, bullets were often still molded individually by the owner of the firearm. . . . Goddard found the bullet buried in the butler's bed headboard and compared it carefully with the butler's own pistol and

bullet mold. He found a raised mark on the bullet that matched a defect in the mold, proving that the shot had been fired from the butler's own weapon.[4]

Faced with the evidence, Randall admitted he had staged the scene. British law enforcement researchers Keith Skinner, Martin Fido, and Alan Moss remarked that, once he was in prison,

> Randall confessed to making up the story with a view to obtaining a reward from his mistress for his bravery in protecting her property, and was eventually released with a sharp warning from the court.[5]

Goddard's case became a milestone in the history of forensics ballistics. His examination of the butler's bullets proved that Randall's weapons had been the source of the evidence found at the scene, and had led to justice being served.

However, this science did not come into its own until the early twentieth century. By that time, law enforcement personnel and prosecutors began to accept the validity of its findings, and its practitioners became involved in more and more court cases. One such landmark case, from the United States, further helped advance the science of forensic ballistics and helped free a man who had been wrongly sentenced to die.

Saved by Science: The Charles Stielow Case

In 1915, Charles Stielow, a German immigrant, was a farmhand on the Phelps farm in rural New York. On March 22, he discovered the body of Margaret Wolcott, the farm's housekeeper, and Charles Phelps, the owner. Both had been shot with a .22 caliber handgun. Wolcott was dead, and Phelps died later that day.

At first, Stielow denied owning a firearm of that size, but his brother-in-law, Nelson Green, confessed to police that

"Every Contact Leaves a Trace"

For law enforcement personnel, and particularly for forensic scientists, every investigation reminds them of the work of Edmond Locard (1877–1966). Locard was a pioneer in forensic science and in criminology who developed a twelve-point matching system for identifying fingerprints, as well as created one of the world's first crime labs, in Lyon, France.

Today, Locard is best remembered for his summation of human interaction and contact. His 1920 statement:

> . . . on the one hand, the criminal leaves marks at the crime scene of his passage; on the other hand, by inverse action, he takes with him, on his body or on his clothing, evidence of his stay or his deed. Left or received, these traces are of extremely varied types.

has become known as "Locard's Exchange Principle."

Many writers and researchers summarize this principle as "Every contact leaves a trace." Although Locard was originally referring to inter-actions between criminals and dust at the scene, modern science allows investigators to look for far more indications of criminal activity than in Locard's day.

Quoted in John Horswell and Craig Fowler, "Associative Evidence—The Locard Exchange Principle," in *The Practice of Crime Scene Investigation.* Boca Raton, FL: CRC Press, 2004 p. 47.

he had hidden several guns for Stielow. Under interrogation, Green confessed that he and Stielow had murdered the house-keeper and farm owner. Stielow also confessed after he was promised by police officers that he could go home to his wife if he admitted to the murders. However, Stielow was not released, and he and Green were charged with murder. In prison, Stielow recanted his confession.

For the court trial, the prosecution hired Albert H. Hamilton, a self-professed firearms expert. His dramatic testimony included photographs of the bullets taken from the victims' bodies. He maintained that the bullets had distinctive scratches that had come from Stielow's gun; although these scratches were not visible in the photos, Hamilton proclaimed that "the bullets that killed the defendant's employer could have been fired by no other weapon."[6] The jury believed him, and both Green and Stielow were convicted. Green received life imprisonment, and Stielow was sentenced to death.

A Second Chance

While on death row, Stielow spoke many times with the prison's deputy warden. The warden became convinced of Stielow's innocence and contacted a humanitarian group on his behalf. They hired private detectives who discovered two other prisoners who had been overheard discussing the murders. One later confessed and then retracted his confession, but it was enough to raise questions about Stielow's guilt. The governor of New York arranged for two detectives, George Bond and Charles Waite, to investigate the case.

Waite took Stielow's gun and the bullets used in the murder to a New York City police detective. The detective compared bullets fired from the gun to the bullets found in the victims, and, contrary to the testimony given by Alfred H. Hamilton, he found that there were significant differences in the scratches on the bullets.

Waite also tried to find the scratches Hamilton had described. According to crime writer Katherine Ramsland, "optics expert Max Poser examined the bullets under a high-powered microscope and could not see any of the alleged scratches that Hamilton had 'observed.'"[7] Bond and Waite concluded that Stielow's gun did not fire the bullets that killed Wolcott and Phelps. When presented with these results, the governor pardoned Stielow and Green. Both had been in prison for over three years, and on at least one occasion, Stielow had been within forty minutes of being executed before a court order halted it.

Charles Waite was so outraged by the injustice of Stielow's case that he spent the rest of his life developing the science of firearms identification, founding the Bureau of Forensic Ballistics in New York City. Following the conclusion of World War I, Waite and a team of scientists set out to prove that even mass-produced firearms left distinctive marks on barrels and projectiles. According to criminalist Keith Inman and consultant Norah Rudin, Waite's team's work on microscopic techniques attracted Calvin Goddard (no relation to London's Henry Goddard), "who led the group's efforts to perfect the comparison microscope, enabling bullets to be compared side-by-side in the same visual field."[8]

Calvin Goddard inspects a gun barrel in the Sacco and Vanzetti investigation.

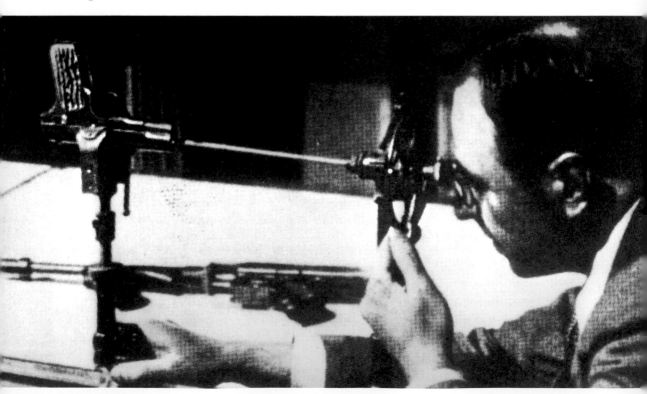

Charles Stielow's case had attracted attention throughout the United States. However, the case of two murder suspects in Massachusetts attracted worldwide attention, and the forensic ballistics evidence played a large part in this landmark case.

Sacco & Vanzetti

On the afternoon of Friday, April 15, 1920, two security guards carrying the payroll for a shoe factory in South Braintree, Massachusetts, were killed by two men, who fled the scene in a car with three other men. Eyewitnesses described the men as "Italian-looking" and that one had a handlebar mustache.

Two suspects, Nicola Sacco and Bartolomeo Vanzetti, were later arrested and charged in the crime, in part because Sacco had in his possession a .32 caliber Colt automatic pistol, which matched the caliber of the murder weapon. In addition, Sacco was also carrying ammunition manufactured by the same company as the casings found at the scene.

Sacco's and Vanzetti's trial began in the summer of 1921, and attracted worldwide attention, in part because of the defendants' political beliefs. (Both were considered to be anarchists, those who believe that all forms of government are undesirable and unnecessary.) But it was the firearms identification evidence that proved to be the pair's undoing.

The Trial, the Verdict, and the Appeals

During the trial, both the prosecution and the defense offered ballistic evidence, based on four bullets that had been recovered from the murdered security guards. While the ballistics experts for the defense were confident in their assertions that the bullets could not have come from Sacco's Colt, the keys to the case turned out to be the cartridges Sacco had had in possession at the time of his arrest. The bullet that had killed one of the guards was such an outdated design that, according to Ramsland, "the only bullets similar to it that anyone could locate to make comparisons were those in Sacco's pockets."[9] The men were convicted and sentenced to death.

Over the next six years, two additional hearings were held concerning the legitimacy of the convictions. The defense hired Albert Hamilton—the same man who had been involved in the Stielow case—in 1923, but his treatment of the evidence failed to sway the presiding judge, and a new trial was not granted. In 1927, a committee appointed to examine the case hired Calvin Goddard, who test-fired Sacco's gun in the presence of an expert hired by the defense. Using a comparison microscope, both men examined the bullet from Sacco's gun along with those recovered at the scene. This visual evidence led the defense expert to agree

Bartolomeo Vanzetti and Nicola Sacco are escorted from jail to the courthouse in 1927 after being found guilty of murder. The Sacco and Vanzetti murder case was a landmark in the field of forensic ballistics.

Recovering a Serial Number

Firearms examiners often are presented with weapons with illegible serial numbers. Criminals try to obliterate these numbers as a way of eliminating part of the evidence trail. However, there are ways to restore this vital information.

1. The forensic examiner determines the make and model of the firearm.

2. The examiner looks up the manufacturer's information to determine the location of the serial number.

3. Assuring that the weapon is unloaded and safe, the examiner disassembles the firearm and locates the serial numbers.

4. The examiner inspects the damaged numbers to determine how the damage was created. The method of damage can dictate the next steps.

5. If a punch or drill has been used, many of the original numbers may be visible using a low-powered stereo microscope. Polishing the surface with wet and dry abrasive paper may reveal more information.

6. The examiner may choose to use a chemical agent to further enhance the serial number. The agent applied depends on the metal of the weapon, and is used to etch into the softer areas of the metal, revealing the serial numbers.

7. The examiner documents all steps with thorough notes and photographs as directed by agency standards.

that the bullets were a match. Sacco and Vanzetti were executed later that year.

The Legacy of Sacco and Vanzetti

The case against Sacco and Vanzetti demonstrated two important developments in the field of forensic ballistics. One was the validity of expert examination; the self-taught experts, such as Albert Hamilton, were being supplanted by individuals such as Charles Waite and Calvin Goddard who were able to reinforce their assertions with evidence that both judge and jury could see and understand.

The second was the increased awareness of law enforcement and judicial personnel concerning firearms. One of the reasons that Hamilton's 1923 evidence failed to sway the presiding judge was that Hamilton had been caught trying to manipulate the evidence. Hamilton had brought three Colt revolvers into the court room; two were new and one was Sacco's. He attempted to prove that Sacco's revolver was not necessarily the murder weapon by disassembling all three revolvers to show their similarities, but when he tried to place the barrel from Sacco's revolver on the body of one of the new ones, Judge Webster Thayer caught him in the act and halted the hearing.

The Sacco and Vanzetti case remains controversial to this day. Some individuals continue to assert that the men were convicted because of their political views or because of their national origins (both had been born in Italy), or both. However, the case is a landmark for forensic ballistics investigations, and helped pave the way for increased use of scientific techniques in the investigation and prosecution of crime.

Pioneers such as Calvin Goddard and Charles Waite continued their work after the Sacco and Vanzetti case was closed. Their work at the Bureau of Forensic Ballistics helped pave the way for mainstream acceptance of forensic ballistics, as well as create a database of firearms characteristics to which law enforcement professionals could refer. In addition, they helped create professionalism in a field that had once been populated

Modern-day forensic ballistics professionals owe a debt of gratitude to those who pioneered the science in the early twentieth

by amateurs. Today's firearms identification professionals follow in their footsteps, continuing the work of collecting and analyzing evidence in order to bring their investigation to a successful conclusion.

CHAPTER 2

Evidence Left Behind

Over the succeeding decades since the Sacco and Venzetti case, law enforcement professionals and scientists from a variety of specialties developed a wide range of techniques that enable them to collect, examine, and quantify evidence at crime scenes. One of their ever-challenging jobs remains to connect evidence to a firearm responsible for a crime, and then to the individual who fired it. But the first link in that chain is the evidence left behind.

Gathering the Evidence

One the morning of March 10, 2008, police in the Philadelphia, Pennsylvania, suburb of Woodbury, New Jersey, investigated a report of two suspicious men. According to local law enforcement officials, the men had been knocking on doors looking for drugs, and a Woodbury resident called 911. Woodbury police caught up with the men outside a donut shop. When one officer stepped out of his patrol car, one of the men, Earl Bernard Harris, thirty-six, of Camden, New Jersey, pulled out a handgun. The officer shot him in the arm and the pelvis; the other man surrendered without incident.

While Harris was flown to a nearby hospital, law enforcement investigators from the Gloucester County's prosecutor's office began their investigation. As with any scene in which a crime may have been committed, law enforcement personnel who investigate shootings need to secure the location to ensure that unauthorized individuals do not enter or disturb the area.

Once the scene is secured, investigators begin to gather and document the evidence left behind. This may involve a number

of specialized personnel, including representatives from the coroner's or medical examiner's office, official photographers to document the scene on film or videotape, and crime scene investigators to check for trace evidence such as fingerprints. In this case, the local prosecutor's office began the investigation because an officer had been involved in the shooting. This ensured that the investigation was carried out by trained staff not employed by the police. This reduces any potential claims of conflicts of interest between the officer involved in the shooting and the investigators.

At a crime scene forensics officers are responsible for collecting all evidence, such as bullet casings, examining gunshot wounds, and looking for the weapon itself.

Additionally, investigators collect any evidence related to the shooting itself. A weapon may have been left behind at the scene, along with spent cartridges. The shooting victim often has bullets still lodged inside his or her body; these cannot be collected except by trained medical personnel in a medical facility. Following the incident, Harris's weapon was recovered at the scene. An official with the Gloucester County Prosecutors

Becoming a Firearms and Toolmarks Examiner

Job Description:
A firearms and toolmarks examiner processes firearms and weapons for the identification and classification of cartridge cases, bullets, and toolmarks for microscopic identification, comparison, and entry into the Integrated Ballistics Identification System. He or she performs gun powder residue pattern tests, proximity tests, and serial number restoration. In addition, a firearms and toolmarks examiner prepares reports and summaries, relays results of tests to investigators, and testifies in court and legal proceedings.

Education:
An increasing number of jurisdictions require professional undergraduate degrees in physical sciences such as chemistry, biology, biochemistry, or physics; some may accept on-the-job experience for lower-graded positions in lieu of a degree.

Qualifications:
Experience with and knowledge of firearms and other types of weapons is necessary. Additional knowledge of computers, police methods, practices and procedures is a plus. Some employers require the individual to hold or obtain a certificate of qualification from the Association of Firearm and Tool Mark Examiners.

Additional Information:
Firearm and toolmark examiners must be self-motivated and able to work independently. They must also have good information gathering and organization skills; critical thinking skills; and the ability to communicate orally and in writing.

Salary:
$40,000 to more than $85,000 per year.

Office said it was a .357 Magnum, a very powerful handgun, and that it had been loaded at the time of the incident.

All evidence related to an investigation, such as the firearm found at the Woodbury donut shop, is carefully recorded and documented when it is found at the scene, as well as throughout its journey to different departments and jurisdictions during analysis. This "chain of custody" practice of securing evidence ensures that all evidence is completely and accurately accounted for, and that all records associated with each piece are up-to-date.

As with many cases, shooting investigations involve trained staff at a crime lab. Crime lab personnel may concentrate on one discipline, such as DNA analysis or surveillance video examination. Others may have expertise in more than one area of study. But each is a highly trained and highly motivated member of the law enforcement community, and in cases involving firearms, they bring a variety of skills and techniques to bear in analyzing the evidence.

> **By the Numbers**
>
> # 14,990
>
> **Number of homicides in the United States in 2006, according to the FBI.**

Analyzing Firearms Evidence

When investigators bring evidence of a shooting to the crime lab, one of the analysts' first tasks is to examine the evidence for distinctive markings that are the result of manufacturing, and for those that are the results of the weapon or weapons firing. These marks exist on shell cartridges and bullets, as well as inside or outside the firearms themselves.

With some cases, such as the investigation into the "D.C. Snipers" shootings, shell casings may be the first solid evidence with which a firearms examiner can work. According to Sari Horwitz and Michael E. Ruane, investigative reporters for the *Washington Post*, the first casing was found at Iran Brown's school: "Scouring the area with rakes, Montgomery County police cadets found a shell casing from a .223 rifle bullet that

A forensic scientist examines a shell casing with aid of a computer at the Miami Regional Crime Lab. He is looking for distinctive markings that would match a bullet to a particular gun or crime scene.

police thought might have been ejected from the shooter's gun."[10] The second was found twelve days later, shortly after Jeff Hopper was shot outside the Ponderosa Steakhouse, by a special agent for the Bureau of Alcohol, Tobacco, Firearms and Explosives (commonly known by the acronyms BATFE or ATF) and his gunpowder-sniffing dog.

These casings provided the investigators with vital evidence. Not all firearms have mechanisms that eject casings automatically; for example, cartridge casings inside revolvers need to be removed by hand. But many modern firearms do contain automatic ejectors, and the casings left behind after the shooter departs contain vital clues about the weapon.

These casings, as well as bullets found at the crime scene and/or recovered from victims, contain vital information called "toolmarks." These distinguishing marks are created when objects made of harder metals come in contact with objects of softer metals. Such information may lead investigators to determine the ammunition's manufacturer, as well as the weapon's make and model.

Identifying Toolmarks Left Behind

The identification of toolmarks is an essential part of firearms identification. The Scientific Working Group for Firearms and Toolmarks is comprised of firearms identification professionals who work to create consistent guidelines for members of their profession. The group, known by the acronym SWGGUN, remarked that whenever a weapon is made, the metal from which it is formed will have unique characteristics left by the tools that created it. In addition, these individualities will be transferred to the softer metal bullets fired from the weapon.

> These irregularities which are formed randomly are considered unique and can individualize or distinguish one tool from another. Because these irregularities or individual characteristics are typically imparted onto the work piece [such as a bullet or cartridge case], the comparative study of the imparted markings allow the tool to be individually associated or identified as having produced the mark.[11]

In the realm of firearms identification, there are a variety of tools that leave such marks. According to Sally A. Schehl of the FBI's Forensic Science Unit:

41

Firing pin impressions, breechface marks, extractor marks, ejector marks, and chamber marks, when present and of sufficient quality, are all features used by firearms examiners in their analyses.[12]

Firing pin impressions occur when the gun's firing pin strikes the base of the shell casing where the primer is located. Each pin is a piece of machine-ground metal, and each has minutely distinct characteristics that may be transferred to the cartridge. Breechface marks are made when the cartridge slams backwards against the rear of the firing chamber, called the "breechface," by the gasses of the burning gunpowder. Once again, the microscopically unique characteristics of this piece of machined metal may be transferred to the shell casing.

Ejector and extractor marks may occur as the cartridge case is mechanically extracted from the chamber and ejected. The resulting marks are fine striations, or scratches, and gouged impressions on the rim and head of the casing. Chamber marks are parallel striations on the cartridge case, and are caused when the shell comes in contact with the walls of the firing chamber inside the firearm.

For the forensic scientist, each mark is a clue to the origin of the ammunition and to the firearm from which it came. In turn, the firearm may perhaps lead investigators to the shooter behind the weapon. But it is with the examination of these toolmarks that forensic firearms identification begins.

"It Took Six Hours"

The examination of toolmarks in firearms identification remains much the same as it was in the days of Charles Waite and Calvin Goddard. According to SWGGUN, the most widely accepted method used in conducting a toolmark examination is "a side-by-

Solving the St. Valentine's Day Massacre

On February 14, 1929, in Chicago, Illinois, seven gang members were murdered in what became known as the "St. Valentine's Day Massacre." The police department theorized that it had been initiated by Chicago's notorious gang leader Al Capone.

The investigators called on Calvin Goddard for his expertise. In 1930, he summarized his findings in the first issue of the *American Journal of Police Science.*

> The very fact that the shells were found in the garage at all was of itself sufficient indication, considering the known circumstances surroundings the shootings, that they were fired in automatic arms.
>
> A study of the rifling marks left upon these bullets showed all to bear the imprint of a barrel rifled with six grooves inclined to the right. . . . All of the bullets removed from the bodies were of .45 automatic pistol type . . . identical in caliber, type, make and vintage with those found on the floor of the garage.

He concluded the killers had used Thompson submachine guns.

In December 1929, Fred Burke, one of Capone's henchmen, was arrested in St. Joseph, Michigan, in connection with the killing of a police officer. Police found two Thompsons and a cache of .45 caliber ammunition at his home. Goddard matched these guns and ammunition to those found at the Chicago massacre, showing that Capone had been behind the shootings. Burke was convicted and sent to prison.

Calvin Goddard, "The Valentine Day Massacre: A Study in Ammunition-Tracing," *American Journal of Police Science*, January-February, 1930. http://www.firearmsid.com/ Feature%20Articles/ stvalentine/index.htm.

In the Washington, D.C., sniper case, firearms expert Evan Thompson testifies how he was able to pinpoint markings on a victim's bullet to marks caused by the shooter's gun barrel, thus determining a match between the two.

side, microscopic comparison of the markings on a questioned material item to known source marks imparted by a tool."[13]

The key to these examinations is the use of a precise and practiced routine. According to Kurt Moline, a forensic scientist with the Minnesota Bureau of Criminal Apprehension, the best way to approach them is "the scientific method. I gather the data, test my assumptions, formulate a conclusion, and present my findings based on the evidence available."[14]

The ATF examiners proceeded in the same manner when they studied the rifle found during the arrest of Lee Boyd Malvo and John Allen Muhammad on October 24, 2002. The seven examiners assigned to the task performed a series of side-by-side comparisons to match bullets fired by the rifle to those associated with the shootings. In his memoir, Charles Moose described the meticulous care that was taken with the evidence:

> The ATF guys were slow and methodical, and tested each bullet and bullet fragment we had, one at a time. When they were done testing them all, and had all their results, the man conducting the forensics experiments stepped aside, another ATF expert came in, and the tests were done all over again from the beginning. They didn't want there to be any possibility of a mistake, or any possibility of doubt, when they were done.[15]

Moose remarked that the examination took "six hours. Six hours! It was a long time to wait,"[16] but in the end, the ATF was able to report that the Bushmaster recovered with Malvo and Muhammad was, indeed, the weapon involved in the shootings.

Studying bullets and bullet fragments is painstaking work. The metals from which they are made are easily scratched, so great care must be taken by the examiner to ensure that no new marks are created. It is essential that the only marks on the bullet are those involved in its firing and its impact, because these can contain the key to discovering from which weapon they were fired. These striations are called "lands" and "grooves."

Lands and Grooves

Whenever a gun barrel has a rifling pattern cut inside it, cutting these grooves leaves "lands," or high parts, intact between them. The spiral lands and grooves give the bullet its spin as it travels down the barrel. As the bullet moves from the firing chamber into the barrel, it comes in contact with the beginning of the land and groove pattern. The spiral pattern of the lands and grooves sends the bullet spinning in the same direction as the rifling cuts. Each manufacturer has a particular cutting pattern, and the direction and the degree of the tilt of each twist will be the same for each particular model of firearm. For example, a .32 caliber Smith and Wesson handgun has five lands and

With modern technology shell casings and bullets can be examined in minute detail to determine their original characteristics, even if the bullet or casing has been damaged.

grooves in a clockwise pattern inside the barrel, which is called a "right twist." By contrast, a .32 caliber Colt has six lands and grooves with a counterclockwise pattern, or a "left twist."

This information is vital to the work of the forensic ballistics investigator. The grooves on a bullet are a reflection of the lands in the gun, and vice versa. However, bullets do not always arrive at the crime lab in pristine condition. Sometimes they are deformed by impact with objects such as bones or buildings. Sometimes these result in the bullet fragmenting in several pieces.

Even if the shell casing or the bullet is in less-than-pristine condition, an investigator can still obtain valuable information. According to Moline, "Given a fragment, I can approximate the bullet's caliber—a .22 will be half the size of a .44—and given at least one land and groove, I can measure its width and angle of twist."[17] This analysis allows examiners to theorize important information about the evidence's original condition. These are called the ammunition's "class characteristics" and "individual characteristics."

Determining Characteristics

In firearms identification, each bullet or shell casing has two sets of characteristics. Class characteristics include the design of a barrel's rifling, such as four grooves with a right twist, the width of lands and grooves, and its caliber. Individual characteristics form a subset of class characteristics. According to Schehl, these are "distinct, unique marks produced during the manufacturing process and include signatures of damage and wear, such as the impression left by a deformed or broken firing pin or the unusual striations left on a bullet by a spur on a sawn barrel."[18]

These features allow examiners to classify items in evidence in comparison to one another, leading to one of three choices. A finding of "identification" exists when the technician finds a match between two ammunition components or a match between an ammunition component and a firearm. An "exclusion," on the other hand, represents no match between the items examined.

Finally, "no conclusion" means that the bullet or casing could be neither conclusively identified nor eliminated as having been fired from a particular weapon. While the class characteristics of a particular piece of evidence may be in agreement with a known sample—the examiner can, for instance, conclusively say the cartridge came from a .44 caliber handgun—there is insufficient evidence to match the evidence's individual characteristics to a particular gun.

Determining class characteristics on a particular piece of evidence will aid law enforcement personnel in their investigations. The class characteristics eliminate a wide range of weapons from consideration, and may help detectives focus on particular individuals who have been associated in the past with the type of weapon in question.

However, given the large number of individual pieces of a particular make and model of a firearm, that can still be a daunting task. That is why determining individual characteristics is much more valuable, and modern computer technology makes this part of the examiner's job a bit easier.

Getting a Hit

After determining the class characteristics of a piece of evidence, Moline consults an FBI database called the General Rifling Characteristics (GRC) File. The file includes lands and grooves information based on samples sent to the FBI by examiners such as Moline from crime labs across the country, and it often enables investigators to determine the make and model of the firearm that fired the original bullet. The file is particularly valuable, according to Moline, "if I have a bullet but no weapon to match it to."[19]

The next step for firearms investigators in the United States is to use the Integrated Ballistics Identification System, or IBIS. IBIS is a computerized digital imaging system that captures digital photographs of fired bullets and cartridge cases. These images are stored in a database and can be electronically compared to other images in the system. IBIS is also connected to the National Integrated Ballistics Information Network (or NIBIN), which is maintained by BATFE. Both IBIS and NIBIN are essential tools for law enforcement personnel, and have led to thousands of "hits" that help investigators connect incidents that may have seemed unrelated.

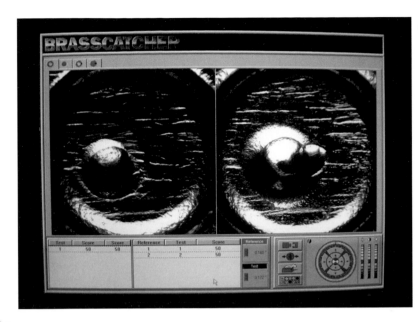

A computer monitor shows the firing pin markings of two different bullets. An image such as this can be stored in the Integrated Ballistics Identification System, or IBIS, and can be electronically compared to other images in the system.

When Moline has a cartridge in evidence, he uses a comparison microscope to photograph the casing's features, and then uploads the information to NIBIN. The network's system then studies the photographs and compares them to others in the database. Because Moline works in Minnesota, he most often requests a link between his questioned cartridge and any others uploaded from other Minnesota investigators. The hope is that his cartridge generates a "hit"— in other words, it correlates to another one already in the network.

> Because correlations are sent out every four hours, we may get a hit in a few minutes if we time it right. Otherwise, it can be up to four hours before we get any hits. And when they come in, we may get as many as 120 images to examine. Larger jurisdictions, like Chicago, have a larger database to examine, and they may get as many as 500 images at a time.[20]

With these hits in hand, the investigator still has to make an additional, side-by-side visual comparison between the original cartridge and the one that is generated through NIBIN. This may be based on the NIBIN images alone, although, Moline pointed out, it is best to "retrieve the original sample from evidence"[21] whenever possible, as photographs may not bring out all the details needed for an accurate comparison.

However, there are times when an investigator may not have the original sample on hand; in some cases, there may not be any shell casings, bullets, or firearms available to analyze. Fortunately, advances in technology have afforded today's crime lab personnel the means to further their efforts to match bullet and casing to gun, and gun to shooter.

NIBIN Makes Connections

The Battle Creek, Michigan, police department used the National Integrated Ballistics Information Network (NIBIN) to link evidence recovered during a drive-by shooting to an arrest of suspects with several outstanding arrest warrants. In early February 2008, Battle Creek officers responded to a call of a report of shots fired. When they arrived, officers met with the residents who indicated that someone drove by and shot at them. Ten shell casings were recovered at the scene and were submitted for entry into NIBIN.

One week later, officers initiated a traffic stop on a vehicle for a traffic violation. The vehicle stopped after a brief attempt to elude the officers. Both male suspects were arrested on various traffic violations and outstanding arrest warrants. Inside the vehicle, officers recovered a plastic baggie of cocaine, open intoxicants, and a weapon. The recovered weapon was submitted for test firing and was imaged into the IBIS system at the police department. The firearm was a match to the ballistic evidence which was recovered during the drive-by shooting that occurred seven days earlier.

Advances in Technology

The modern crime lab bears little resemblance to the ones established during Calvin Goddard's career. While the comparison microscope continues to be an invaluable tool, it has been joined by a number of other instruments that play important roles in the crime lab's work. In addition, forensic firearms investigators may need to master more than the fine art of making visual comparisons. Their work often takes them into the world of chemistry, metallurgy, and computer technology.

One area of firearms identification that has evolved since the 1970s is the detection of gunshot residue, or GSR. Early investigators understood that when a weapon is fired, residue from the combustion of the powder and primer is often found on the skin or clothing of the shooter, the victim, or both. Historically, investigators tested for GSR using simple tests, such as applying paraffin wax or tape on suspected surfaces. However, more modern tests by crime lab personnel use chemical analysis and X-ray microscopy to test for GSR.

Gunshot Residue Analysis

The best time for testing for GSR is at the scene, when law enforcement personnel can obtain samples from the skin and clothing of individuals they believe were involved in the incident. However, GSR evidence can be lost or destroyed if evidence connected to the incident is not properly preserved. The simple act of washing one's hands or clothing may remove important GSR evidence. In addition, GSR evidence is present only when a handgun is used; by the time a bullet leaves a rifle, or pellets leave a shotgun, the residue is left behind inside the barrel. Consequently, investigators take as many samples as possible for future testing while at the scene, because, according to Edward C. Klatt, of the Department of Pathology at the University of Utah, "primer residue may be found in targets or wounds at considerable distance from the muzzle (up to 200 meters)."[22]

Conducting a GSR Test

Proper collection of evidence is a critical step in building a case against a criminal. Police officers, detectives, and crime scene investigators follow steps to make certain that evidence can be used in court. These steps are recommended in the United States Department of the Treasury's handbook on crime scene and evidence collection:

1. Wash your hands or put on a pair of latex gloves.

2. Moisten two cotton swabs in dilute (5 percent) nitric acid and thoroughly swab the back of the suspect's right hand.

3. Place swabs in a plastic bag and label with your initials, the date and exhibit number.

4. Repeat the above process for the right palm, the back of the left hand and the left palm areas of the suspect's hand.

5. If use of a rifle or shotgun is suspected, swab both right and left cheeks of the face.

6. If a spent casing is available, swab the interior using plain water (not acid), place swab in plastic bag and label the bag "casing."

7. Package articles of clothing to be tested for gunshot residue separately in plastic bags.

The key to GSR testing is understanding the chemistry of ammunition. Primer and gunpowder are composed of certain chemical elements and in certain proportions. The major components of primer are lead, barium, or antimony; usually, all three are present. The basic ingredient for many types of modern gunpowder is a highly flammable compound called

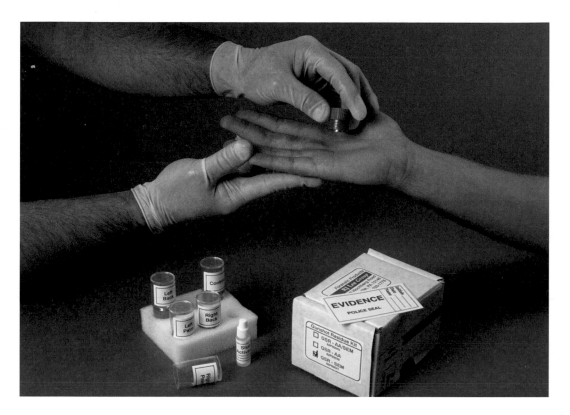

nitrocellulose. Other recipes use nitrocellulose and up to 40 percent nitroglycerine, and may contain up to twenty additional organic compounds.

One of the most effective techniques in testing for GSR is called "scanning electron microscopy with energy dispersive analysis" (or SEM-EDA). The technician uses a scanning electron microscope and energy dispersive X-ray spectrometer to perform detailed surface analysis as well as high magnification viewing of very small features.

The most advantageous use of the SEM spectrometer occurs when other evidence is missing, including bullets, casings, or the gun itself. When the SEM-EDA system creates an analysis of the elements within the sample, it recognizes the elements found in primer and gunpowder, and therefore can demonstrate that the surface tested did contain GSR.

The SEM system is also useful when bullets or cartridges are present. According to Moline, the samples may contain

When a gun is fired, gunshot residue, or GSR, is left behind on the shooter's hands and clothes. Here, evidence is collected from a person's hand to be tested for gunshot residue.

evidence of other materials, such as bone fragments, "that show up in the initial analysis, so that we know to send them to [the] DNA [technician] for study before we work on the toolmarks."[23]

The combination of GSR analysis and toolmarks examination may lead the investigators to particular individuals they theorize may be involved in the shooting. Their work in the lab, however, is only one part of a forensic firearms investigation. Additional measurements and analyses take place at the scene of the incident and behind a computer, as technicians and detectives work to uncover what exactly happened before, during, and after a weapon was fired.

CHAPTER 3

The Flight of a Bullet

Anyone who has ever tried to throw an American football knows that there are many ways to do it, but only one way is the most efficient. Unlike a baseball, softball, or soccer ball, which are spheres without a definite front or back, the football's pointed ends affect how it moves through the air. While a baseball and other spheres will spin while in flight, a football will tumble end over end if not given the proper spin around its middle, and, therefore, will not fly effectively toward its target.

Once a bullet is fired, a number of factors can impact its trajectory, or direction, speed, and spin.

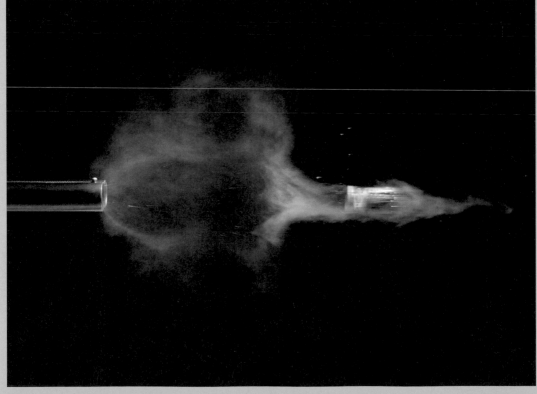

Such is also the case with bullets. Once they leave the muzzle of the firearm, the rifled barrel gives them the spin they need to travel efficiently. However, a variety of forces may affect the bullet's spin and direction, called its "trajectory," including its original speed, gravity, and wind. In addition, other objects may come in contact with the bullet and change its trajectory. Its ultimate resting spot—where its trajectory ends—is dictated by all these factors, and is governed by what scientists call the laws of motion.

The Laws of Motion

Sir Isaac Newton (1642–1727) was an English mathematician, physicist, and astronomer. He is remembered for a number of scientific achievements, but crime scene investigators examining the scene of a shooting deal with two of Newton's Laws of Motion. These statements help explain in general terms how bodies act when they are in motion, and each applies to how bullets fly when they are shot from a weapon.

Newton's first law can be summarized by the statement that an object will stay at rest, or will continue to move at a constant velocity, unless some force is applied to it. In terms of firearms ballistics, this simply means that a bullet does not move until some force is applied to it. The force placed upon the bullet to send it spinning down the gun barrel is the expanding gas from the combustion of the primer and gunpowder. The bullet will continue moving until some other force is exerted upon it, such as gravity, or it encounters another object with a greater mass that stops its flight, such as a wall or a body.

Newton's third law is usually paraphrased as, "For every action, there is an equal and opposite reaction." When it comes to firearms, the reaction that occurs when a weapon is fired is called recoil; the amount of recoil felt by a shooter is based on the amount of energy expended by the powder charge and the mass of the bullet. Because the mass of the shooter plus the gun is considerably greater than the mass of the bullet, the amount of force exerted on those two masses is considerably less than what is exerted on

the bullet. Consequently, the bullet will travel far further than the shooter's arm will move due to recoil.

These laws of motion explain how bullets perform in general. However, the dynamics of bullets are also determined by several other factors, including the type of weapon that fired it and its eventual resting spot. The study of bullets in motion can be further broken down into three categories: "internal," "external," and "terminal" ballistics.

Bullets in Motion

Every object that moves interacts with the environment around it. For firearms investigators, internal ballistics refers to the

Whenever a weapon is fired, the shooter experiences a force called recoil. The amount of recoil felt by a shooter is based on the amount of energy expended by the powder charge and the mass of the bullet.

study of the ammunition while it is still inside the weapon, from the time the primer is ignited to the time the bullet leaves the barrel's muzzle. The study involves the size of the round as well as the amount and type of powder used in the cartridge.

External ballistics covers the behavior of the bullet while it is in flight; terminal ballistics deals with the bullet's penetration of anything denser than air. Retired Albuquerque, New Mexico, sergeant Guy Pierce describes external ballistics as "any intervening objects that get in the way of the bullet's flight—anything that can change its trajectory—such as a wall."[24] This contact "may send the bullet tumbling before it strikes the target"[25] as well as change its course.

One That Almost Got Away

Clayton Spencer, of Great Britain's Criminal Investigation Division, recalled looking for a bullet for two days at a shooting scene along a busy street before the division was forced to reopen the area on a Friday. The victim had had a bullet pass completely through his body, but the bullet was nowhere to be found at the scene.

Spencer and his colleagues made a meticulous search of the scene, including the ground around the incident, the nearby wall that had been 6 feet (2m) behind the victim, and even down the street's storm drains. But it was nowhere to be found.

Three days later, a young boy came into the police station, "pushing his bike ahead of him. He'd been away for the weekend, come home, taken his bike out of the shed, found the tire flat and there, right there, in the rubber tire, was our slug. Kid had ridden right through the scene—didn't even know that the chap had been shot, just zipped right on by."

Quoted in N.E. Genge, *The Forensic Casebook: The Science of Crime Investigation.* New York: Ballantine Books, 2002, p. 11.

The intervening object often decreases the bullet's velocity, which may affect the end result of the weapons fire, which is known as the bullet's terminal ballistics. This occurs once the bullet strikes an object that is more massive than the bullet itself and its flight ceases.

Each of these factors contributes to the investigation of a shooting. During any crime scene investigation, law enforcement personnel endeavor to reconstruct the incident; they need to determine who was involved, what occurred, where it occurred, and when it occurred. Eyewitness accounts may contribute to each of these, but occasionally are in conflict with each other. Therefore, the investigators rely on scientific methods to formulate their theories. In shooting investigations, one of the key factors that must be analyzed is the trajectory of all bullets involved.

> **By the Numbers**
>
> # 2,600
>
> **Speed (feet per second) at which a .38 caliber bullet travels (792.5 meters per second).**

Trajectory Analysis

In many ways, crime scene investigations are jigsaw puzzles, in which various pieces need to be fitted together in a particular way in order to create the scene of the crime—the accurate picture of what happened. Unlike most jigsaw puzzles, however, trajectory analysis always works in three dimensions. This is because in addition to their horizontal flight, bullets can fly up and down and may turn to the left or right due to an intervening object.

Consider, for example, the shooting that occurred in Wichita, Kansas, on April 27, 2007. Xavier Worley was shot three times outside his apartment; inside, his pregnant girlfriend, Laquishia Starr, had also been shot. The job for law enforcement was to determine if the shootings were related, how many shots had been fired, and if the shots had been fired from the same gun.

Investigators determined that just three shots had done the damage. According to Kansas state prosecutor C.J. Rieg,

To obtain the most accurate representation of a bullet's trajectory, a 3-D reconstruction of the crime scene, as shown here, is commonly used by investigators.

the trajectory analysis revealed noteworthy external and terminal ballistics. Two bullets struck Worley on his left side and one struck him on his right side. "One of those bullets went through him, went through the door, and hit Laquishia Starr right in the head—right between the eyes."[26] Both Starr and the baby later died.

For investigators, piecing together the ballistics evidence in a crime such as this lends important information to the case. Pierce noted that a wide range of conditions needed to be considered when investigating the trajectory ballistics involved in the Wichita shooting:

> You would need to consider the height of the man, as well as the height of the woman, and how tall she was when she was seated on the couch—how far her head was above the floor—and how far the couch was depressed when she was seated on it.[27]

In shooting cases such as this one, there was at least one hole in an intervening object. In many cases, such as the Wichita shooting, investigators find holes in various objects inside a crime scene location. Bullets often penetrate and become lodged inside walls, both inside and outside buildings, and these holes enable the examiners to apply the scientific method to determine how the shooting occurred.

Finding the Shooter's Location

Crime scene specialists who work in incident reconstruction use a variety of tools to determine a shooter's location. Sometimes, the location is easily determined. If shell casings are found on the ground in an area that is directly visible from a wall where

Face to Face?

Retired Albuquerque, New Mexico, sergeant Guy Pierce recalled a case that he helped investigate in which Albuquerque police found a victim with two bullet impacts that baffled them. Eyewitness accounts of an incident between two men said that the two men had been facing each other, but the victim's wounds seemed to contradict the eyewitness statements. One eyewitness observation, and computer-based recreation software, provided the key to understanding the shooting.

> The victim had a bullet wound to the crown of his head; the bullet had passed through his skull and had exited in his mouth, but had not fallen out. The other wound was to the back of his right shoulder blade. . . .
>
> One of the witnesses said he was charging at the shooter, like he was going to tackle him. Once we had that observation, we could recreate the scene [with the program]. Because the victim was bending over, the program showed that the shots lined up with the victim's wounds.

Telephone interview with Guy Pierce, April 7, 2008.

bullet holes are located, investigators will first theorize that the shooter was standing where the casings were found. However, other factors need to be taken into account, including the elevation of surrounding objects.

Given the trajectory evidence at the Wichita scene, Pierce theorized that both Worley and the shooter were standing at the same relative elevation. "If the shooter had been standing on the ground and the victim had been standing on steps outside the door, the angle of the shots would have resulted in the shots being directed upwards."[28] If that had been the case, the bullet that passed through Worley would not likely have hit Starr, seated on the couch inside. Instead, it might have struck the wall behind her or the wall above her. In fact, according to Ron Sylvester, a reporter for the *Wichita Eagle* who covered the trial of the accused shooter, Worley was standing on a "stoop, a concrete slab, [and] Starr was seated inside."[29]

Finding the shooter's location is often more complex. Sometimes no casings are found at the scene. In other cases, there may have been more than one shooter, or there may have been an exchange of gunfire from multiple directions and

Finding the location of a shooter is not always easy. Investigators often have to use bullet holes in windows or doors, or other objects, to help determine where the shooter was standing.

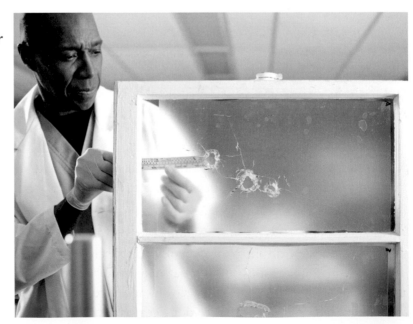

locations. Investigators closely examine holes in walls or in other objects that are known to have been stationary at the time, such as parked vehicles, and using geometric measurements, they can theorize where the shooter stood.

By the Numbers

1,253

According to the FBI, number of homicides in the United States in 2006 of individuals between the ages of 17 and 19.

To aid their calculations, investigators carefully place rods inside the holes. The angle of the rod represents the angle at which the bullet entered the object. These rods are often aluminum, and come in various diameters to represent different calibers of bullets. Some commercially-available kits come with rods that can be assembled into greater lengths by screwing ends together, but other investigators make their own rods. Pierce recalled that he "bought a set of wooden dowels that worked just as well. I painted them bright orange so that they showed up well in our [crime scene] photographs."[30]

A single rod in a single bullet hole may provide enough information for investigators to theorize where the shooter stood. More holes will, of course, provide more information, and in the best case scenario, the rods will create the open end of a cone that leads back to where the shooter was located.

Other cases present greater challenges. Shots that travel great distances before impact are more easily studied with lasers than with rods. Rods are impractical over distances more than a yard (1m) because they will bend under their own weight. Lasers also allow investigators to study trajectories of multiple shooters, as well as trace trajectories through objects that affect the external ballistics.

Lasers provide investigators the opportunity to test their theories about shooter locations over dozens, if not hundreds, of meters in distance. These tools allow law enforcement to recreate shootings where there are no apparent weapons in the vicinity, enabling them to test their theories about what may have happened. As Pierce put it, "You have to be creative when reconstructing a scene—you have to be able to use your imagination."[31]

Creative Thinking in Action

It was this creative thinking skill that helped investigators piece together the "D.C. Snipers" shootings. The low angles from which the shots came had led investigators to theorize that the shooter or shooters had been crouching or lying down when the shots were fired, but they had found no physical evidence of this, such as disturbed foliage, at the scenes. However, when Malvo and Muhammad were apprehended at a rest stop, investigators discovered that the back seat of their Caprice had a special hinge that allowed them to enter and exit the trunk, where the Bushmaster rifle was found. As they had imagined, the shots were being fired from just a short distance above the ground.

Other cases require creative thinking and a bit of knowledge of the people in the area. On March 24, 2008, seventy-one-year-old Mary Keesy was in her back yard in rural Shiloh, Ohio, when she heard four bangs, which she thought had come from rabbit hunters on the outskirts of the town of seven hundred. Then she felt something on top of her head, and when she reached under her nylon head scarf, she found she'd been struck by a bullet. According to Paul Thomas of Cleveland's WKYC-TV:

> Richland County deputies thought someone may have been shooting from a nearby water tower. Then deputies found two 17-year-old boys with rifles about a mile [1.6 kilometers] away from Keesy's house. The teens told deputies that they were shooting into the air. The rifles and shell casings were taken into evidence. The boys are facing misdemeanor, negligent assault charges.[32]

Keesy had some advice for the teen suspects: "Just don't be playing around with those rifles and those guns and be shooting up towards town."[33]

Mary Keesy is one of the lucky ones. Not all shooting victims survive with nothing more than a four-inch (10cm) gash on the scalp. Other shooting victims require much more medical attention, and may not be able to take an active part in the investigators' efforts. In addition, many other shooting victims die from their wounds. However, their bodies still can contain clues as to what occurred.

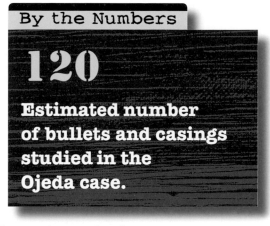

By the Numbers

120

Estimated number of bullets and casings studied in the Ojeda case.

The Victim's Tale

When a shooting victim requires medical attention, trained personnel may not be present in order to take measurements of the bullet's paths into, and sometimes out of, the body. The medical personnel are more concerned with treating the severity of the wounds. If the victim recovers, investigators may be able to theorize where the bullet originated from based on the victim's recollections.

However, if the victim dies, the investigation is turned over to either a coroner or a medical examiner, depending on the jurisdiction. These investigators may also use rods to take measurements to determine the bullet's path and its angle of entry, and their information is then turned over to the investigative authorities.

The key to investigating shootings in which victims are involved is understanding that people will react to getting shot. They may fall down where they are shot, or they may be able to walk or crawl to another location. Wichita's Xavier Worley was not only able to return inside his apartment after being shot, but, once he found that Starr had been hit also, he called 911 from his cell phone and went to the building next door to tell a friend what had happened.

Other victims may have been in motion when they were shot. All of these reactions pose a challenge for investigators trying to piece together the ballistics evidence. The investigators' analyses are complicated further when there

While medical attention is the first priority for shooting victims, some may still be able to provide clues to investigators about the shooting depending on the severity of their injuries.

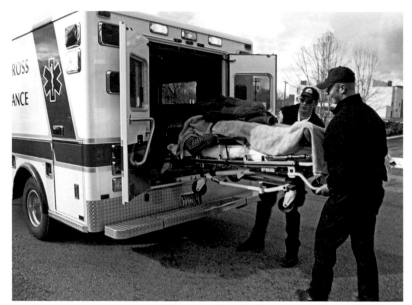

are multiple shooters involved, and when shots are fired from multiple locations. One such situation in Puerto Rico involved FBI personnel and a fugitive from justice.

A Siege in Puerto Rico

In September 2005, FBI personnel intended to capture and arrest Filiberto Ojeda Ríos, a member of the "Macheteros" ("Cane-Cutters"), a group that advocates independence of Puerto Rico by armed struggle from the United States. Ojeda was a fugitive, based on his convictions for a Connecticut bank robbery and on a number of weapons charges. The FBI received credible evidence that Ojeda was living in a small town in western Puerto Rico, and on September 22, 2005, they moved to apprehend him.

Ojeda opened fire almost as soon as the agents arrived; one agent was wounded in the process. Over the next two days, attempts to end the incident peacefully were tried and failed, leading to more gunfire. Other agents were hit but were uninjured because they were wearing bullet-proof equipment. When the agents finally entered the house on the 24th, Ojeda was found dead in his kitchen.

While the U.S. Office of the Inspector General (OIG) conducted interviews with the FBI personnel involved in the siege, the Puerto Rico Institute of Forensic Sciences performed an autopsy, trajectory analyses, and bullet and shell casing examinations. The institute's findings were based solely on the forensic evidence. According to the OIG:

> The Institute found that . . . three rounds passed through the kitchen window, penetrated the left side of the refrigerator, and exited the front of the refrigerator. Two of the shots presented impacts or final penetrations within the residence, while the third (the round that struck Ojeda) did not. The third trajectory exited the refrigerator . . . at a height of 49 inches [1.24 meters], which the Institute found to coincide with the position of the bullet wound on Ojeda's body, assuming a crouched position. From these facts, the Institute concluded that Ojeda was behind the refrigerator when he was struck by the shot, and that he was most likely in a position about one step away from the refrigerator toward the living room at the moment of impact.[34]

The analysis of the three shots through the kitchen window demonstrates the value of determining external and terminal ballistics. The institute recognized the window and the refrigerator as intervening objects, with only the refrigerator likely to have altered the bullet's ballistics. Two of the three shots impacted inside the kitchen, and the terminal ballistics of the third proved fatal for Ojeda.

The investigation studied over 120 bullets and casings, as well as related impacts inside and outside the home. In the past, such examinations were extremely labor-intensive and required multiple geometric measurements and applications. However, advances in computer software have made this aspect of crime scene investigation more productive and less time-consuming.

Software-Based Reconstructions

Recent developments in computer applications now offer law enforcement personnel a wide variety of tools that enable them to investigate incidents. Based on measurements made at the scene, programs will generate trajectory analyses that aid investigators in determining the presumed location of the weapon when it was fired. Pierce uses one such program in his consulting work, and says it has enabled him to create reconstructions of crime scenes that would have been impractical, if not impossible, to recreate otherwise.

These programs also help investigators reconstruct incidents such as the one in Puerto Rico, in which dozens of rounds were fired from multiple directions, both inside and outside a structure, and in which one of the shooters (Ojeda) was not available to add his testimony to the investigation. As a routine part of all investigations, statements are taken from all individuals, including how many shots were fired and by whom, and this information contributes to the program's reconstruction of the events. The information is entered as data points into the computer program, and the program generates trajectory estimates, which can then be modified as more information becomes available.

The most powerful programs have additional tools that aid investigators in examining all angles of their theories. Users can manipulate the three-dimensional model of the scene, such as a room or an alley, so that they can view the scene from above, the side, and any angle in between. Investigators can also create animated movies that allow them to study how the individuals involved may have acted when impacted by the bullets. The animations can have individuals or vehicles in motion while shots are fired, and users can zoom in and out of the scene for better study.

This sophisticated software is also aiding both professional and amateur investigators in recreating and studying one of the most famous shootings of the twentieth century. With the aid of computers that only existed in science fiction at the time,

individuals from around the world recreate and theorize about the 1963 assassination of U.S. president John F. Kennedy.

A virtual reality crime scene reconstruction can aid forensics investigators with their case.

The Assassination of President Kennedy

President Kennedy was killed in Dallas, Texas, on November 22, 1963, as he, his wife, and Texas governor John Connally and his wife rode in a motorcade through Dealey Plaza. According to the official government investigation of the incident, known as the Warren Report, President Kennedy was killed through the actions of one man, Lee Harvey Oswald, who used a high-powered rifle to shoot from the sixth floor

Dale K. Myers's Findings

Veteran animator Dale K. Myers's recreation of the assassination of John F. Kennedy on November 22, 1963, has been shown on several documentaries, including an episode of PBS' *Frontline* called "Who Was Lee Harvey Oswald?" Myers believes that his recreation proves that Oswald was the lone gunman at the scene, and that his trajectory analysis points directly to Oswald's location.

His computer models create trajectory cones for the shots, and each leads back to four windows in the Texas School Book Depository.

> Photographs [from November 22, 1963] show two of the four were open at the time of the shooting. The open window on the fifth floor was occupied by eyewitnesses. The sniper's nest window—the southeast corner, sixth floor—is the only open, unaccounted for window that lies within the area defined by the trajectory cone. This is the location where eyewitnesses saw a rifle being fired from, and where Dallas police later found three spent rifle shells.

Dale K. Myers, "Secrets of a Homicide: Summary of Conclusions." Milford, MI: Oak Cliff Press, 2008. http://www.jfkfiles.com/jfk/html/concl2b.htm.

of a nearby building, the Texas School Book Depository. Another government-initiated study, the 1978–1979 House Select Committee on Assassinations, also concluded that Oswald had acted alone.

Over the years, many have speculated about the events in Dallas. Some have theorized that Oswald did not act alone; that he was not the only gunman at the scene; or that it would have been impossible for Oswald to hit the moving motorcade with three shots from such a great distance. Interested parties from around the world have pored over eyewitness statements, photographic and film evidence, and the Warren Report's findings, to support their various theories.

It is therefore not surprising that researchers have taken advantage of the development of the computer in their quests. Continuing advances in computer modeling, including ballistic and trajectory analysis, have been used to examine and reconstruct the events of November 22, 1963.

Examining Evidence from New Angles

In 1992, an accident and failure investigations company, now called Exponent, used three-dimensional modeling to recreate the assassination. It based its modeling on the layout of Dealey Plaza as well as how Oswald's rifle behaved under normal firing operations. The animation was developed for the American Bar Association's mock trial "The United States v. Lee Harvey Oswald." The result, while visually compelling, was created with the premise that the shots were fired from the sixth floor window of the Texas School Book Depository. Its intent was to demonstrate that President Kennedy's wounds could only have been inflicted by Oswald, the defendant in the mock trial.

However, greater computing power in everyday applications has led to another re-creation that examines the event from a variety of angles and perspectives. Veteran computer animator Dale K. Myers spent nearly ten years creating a digital recreation of the motorcade route and of the film taken by amateur photographer Abraham Zapruder, which seems to best document the assassination. Myers's modeling allows him to not only recreate the Zapruder film, but also examine the events from multiple angles and directions, and in three dimensions.

Myers concluded that both the photographic evidence and the physical evidence of President Kennedy's wounds

This is the approximate view the assassin of President John F. Kennedy might have had through his rifle sight. This scene, using real people, was reconstructed in 1964 during the assassination investigation. In the 1990s and 2000s, computer modeling has been used to examine and reconstruct the events of November 22, 1963.

demonstrate that the shots came from just one location—where Oswald's rifle casings were found in the Texas School Book Depository.

While Myers is not a crime scene investigator or reconstruction specialist, he is a recognized expert on the assassination. He has produced award-winning documentaries about the event and has consulted with various media companies on their productions since the 1980s. His expertise in computer imaging and animation, and his in-depth knowledge of the events of November 22, 1963, has contributed to the field of crime scene investigations. The complete truth of what happened in Dallas may never be known, but his work may have shed some more light on the mystery.

CHAPTER 4

After the Impact

Law enforcement personnel face a hierarchy of priorities when they first arrive at a crime scene in which a shooting is involved. Along with securing the scene and collecting evidence, they need to determine if any victims require medical attention, and, if so, how urgent those needs are. They rely on the expertise of medical personnel to help save the victims' lives, but also to preserve and document as much of the evidence related to the shooting as possible.

The victims' clothing needs to be preserved, as it may contain traces of GSR. Any bullets extracted from the victims need to be handled with extreme care in order to preserve the toolmarks. In addition, the medical personnel contribute to the investigation through their documentation of the wounds inflicted by the bullets. In this way, they are assisting the investigators' analysis of the incident's terminal ballistics. This branch of terminal ballistics is known as "wound ballistics." The character and nature of the victims' wounds are an essential part of the investigation.

The Bullet's Diary

Edward Klatt of the University of Utah observed that wound patterns fall into several general categories, but that "each bullet keeps a diary in its own way of where it has been and what it has done."[35] It is up to the forensic investigators to examine each wound and, as it were, read the diary of the bullet's activity in order to understand its origin and its terminal ballistics.

All firearm-related wounds fall into two basic categories: entrance and exit wounds. An entrance wound is created when

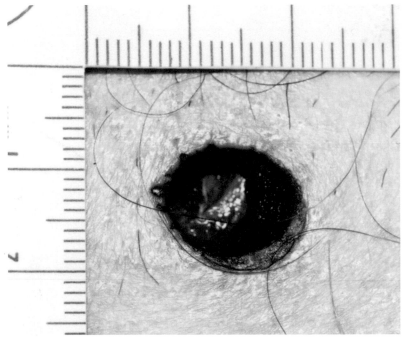

An examination of a bullet wound can tell an investigator many things, including, but not limited to, the type of weapon used, the distance of the muzzle of the weapon from the victim, and the angle at which the bullet entered the body.

a projectile or projectiles enter the body; an exit wound is caused upon leaving the body. An entrance wound varies in size and appearance based on a number of factors. These include the type of weapon that was used, the distance of the muzzle of the weapon from the victim, the caliber and velocity of the bullet, the angle at which the bullet entered the body, and whether or not the bullet passed completely through the victim.

The bullet's diary also includes contact with intervening objects, which may send the bullet tumbling through the air before coming in contact with a victim. Additionally, bullets may begin to yaw (a motion in which the nose of the bullet moves left and right) in the air and continue inside the body. They may also begin or continue to tumble once inside the body.

It is important to remember that because of the conditions under which the wound was received, the size of an entry wound may give misleading information about the bullet. The entrance hole on a victim's clothing may have clean edges and a perfectly round shape, or it may have widespread tearing with jagged edges and no distinct center.

Becoming a Forensic Scientist

Job Description:
A forensic scientist performs complex laboratory analyses on physical evidence, identifying and comparing evidence through a variety of scientific methods, including microscopy, trace amount measurement, and substance analysis. He or she devises analytical approaches to casework that may include research, generating or modifying methods, and interprets analytical results. In addition, a forensic scientist assists law enforcement agencies in processing crime scenes through documenting and protecting evidence according to laboratory procedures, prepares written reports, and testifies as an expert witness in courts of law.

Education:
Minimum requirements usually are a bachelor's degree in a natural science such as biology, chemistry, biochemistry, physics, forensic science, pharmacology, or a closely related field.

Qualifications:
Experience with and knowledge of various scientific testing methods, such as DNA, firearms and toolmarks, and trace evidence. Higher-level positions require increased experience in a laboratory setting.

Additional Information:
Forensic scientists are subject to handling firearms, broken glass, syringes, blood, urine, and other potentially hazardous samples, and may be required to work with caustic and flammable fluids. Forensic scientists are also expected to be self-motivated and detail-oriented; possess good information gathering and organization skills, as well as critical thinking skills; and have the ability to communicate orally and in writing.

Salary:
$30,000 to more than $65,000 per year.

Similarly, when the bullet impacts the living tissue of the victim directly, the size of the entry wound will be sometimes considerably larger than the projectile that caused it. For example, a .38 caliber round striking a body will generally cause an entry wound of approximately 3 inches (7.6cm) in diameter—considerably larger than the 38/100ths of an inch (9.65mm) of the projectile. But one of the most essential tools in reading the bullet's diary is to understand not only the size of the entry wound, but also the markings around it.

By the Numbers

163

Speed (feet per second) at which a bullet must travel to penetrate human skin (49.7 meters per second).

Tears, Smudges, and Stars

Wounds generated by bullets fired from handguns or rifles create distinctive markings on the body. If the weapon's muzzle is two or more feet (0.6m) from the victim, the entrance wound usually is a small hole, with what is called an abrasion collar, in which the skin displays a blue-black ring of bruising around the point of entry. The wound might also have a black smudge around it; this is caused by the skin cleaning the bullet of its burned gunpowder, grime, and oil residue that it accumulated during its passage through the barrel.

A muzzle located between 6 inches (15cm) and 2 feet (0.6m) from the point of entry generates a tattooed or stippled affect on the skin. This is caused by GSR that is discharged from the muzzle and that becomes embedded in the skin, causing tiny hemorrhages inside the skin in a speckled pattern around the wound.

Finally, if the muzzle was less than 6 inches (15cm) from the victim when the weapon was fired, hot gasses and particulate matter are driven directly in to the skin. This chars and rips the skin into a star-shaped pattern.

Each of these marks appears on the victim's skin, but bullets also come in contact with clothing before impacting or penetrating the body. An analysis of the marks left on clothing as well as the wounds on the body provides important information about the incident.

Behind Closed Doors

On the evening of April 25, 2004, police were called to an apartment building in Portland, Oregon, after shots were fired. Stuart Janncy (not his real name), twenty-one, was found dead inside. His roommate, Karl O'Bryan (also a pseudonym), twenty-four, was arrested at the scene, but was fully cooperative with the police, saying he wanted to explain the incident. O'Bryan said that Janney had been physically abusive on many occasions; on this night, Janney had been intoxicated and began striking him. He said he had feared for his life, and that he had shot Janney with his .45 semiautomatic handgun in self-defense.

An analysis of the wounds on the victim, and an analysis of the clothing Janney wore, provided valuable information in the investigation. The autopsy was conducted at the state medical examiner's office, and five bullets were recovered from Janney's body. Each was consistent with the .45 recovered at the scene.

The medical examiner determined that the bullets had entered at an upward angle into Janney's torso, chest, and right arm. There were a variety of wound patterns on the body. For example, two wounds on Janney's left side had no stippling or smudges, but corresponding holes on his shirt had gunshot residue that suggested the weapon was anywhere from 16 to 20 inches (40.5 to 51cm) from the shirt. However, the wound on the right arm had stippling about 4 inches (10cm) in diameter, suggesting the weapon had been less than a few inches—maybe 15 centimeters or less—from Janney during discharge.

Additionally, a hole in the left arm of Janney's T-shirt suggested that a shot had gone through the shirt, missed the arm, and then impacted his left side. The

By the Numbers

213

Speed (feet per second) at which a bullet must travel to break human bone (64.9 meters per second).

For Investigators Only

The University of Tennessee's National Forensic Academy is a unique intensive ten-week program that trains law enforcement officers in evidence identification, collection, and preservation. The students take classes in Knoxville, using a curriculum developed by leading forensic practitioners from across the United States. Students enrolled in the program are trained in and challenged by the various disciplines of forensic science through classroom instruction, lab activities, and field exercises in such specialized courses as evidence processing, burial recovery, bombs and booby traps, arson investigation, and blood-spatter analysis. Academy students complete written and practical exams to demonstrate their mastery of the subject areas. The goal of the academy is to prepare the crime scene investigator to recognize key elements and to improve the process of evidence recovery and submission.

hole in the shirt was surrounded by 1 inch (2.5cm) of dense gunpowder residue, which occurs during a close contact discharge. Janney's wounds, the evidence on his clothing, and the retrieval of .45 caliber bullets from his body (that were the same caliber as O'Bryan's weapon) contributed to the investigators' decision. O'Bryan was charged with Janney's murder, despite his claims of self-defense.

The use of a handgun in the Portland apartment created very distinctive wounds on Janney's body. However, a different weapon would have created a much different series of wounds. While wounds created by handguns and rifles are similar in appearance, shotgun wounds are distinctive in appearance. Because shotgun pellets are loosely packed with a small amount of fabric (called wadding) inside a shotgun cup, they act differently from bullets when ejected from the muzzle and when they separate from the cup in flight. These aspects create unique wound patterns and present special challenges for investigators.

Unique Shotgun Wound Patterns

Understanding wound patterns that may have been caused by a shotgun begins with understanding the shot's behavior. According to crime scene reconstructionist Lucien C. Haag:

> Shotguns present special challenges to crime scene investigators, medical examiners, and firearms examiners. This is largely due to the great variety and complexity of this type of ammunition compared to bulleted cartridges. . . . One of the frustrating aspects of shotgun shootings is that it is very seldom possible to identify shot pellets as having been fired from a particular shotgun.[36]

However, because the wound patterns they create are distinct from those created by bullets, these appearances will greatly aid a shooting investigation.

As with bullet wounds, the distance that the shotgun was from the victim determines the type of wound the shot creates. However, one of the keys to understanding shotgun wounds is the dynamics of the shotcup. The shotcup has four flaps enclosing the pellets, and shortly after the shotgun is discharged and the cup leaves the barrel, the flaps encounter air resistance and begin to open like the petals of a flower after three to four feet (0.9m to 1.2m).

If the shotgun was fired this close to the victim, this behavior will create a distinguishing wound that Haag calls "petal slap." An investigator will not only observe the entry wound as the shot pellets hit the skin in a tight ball but the impact of one or more of the flared petals surrounding the wound. This distinctive marking may also be displayed on the victim's clothing.

A further distinction of shotgun wound impacts will assist the investigator in determining the origin of the pellets. According to Haag, many American shotgun manufacturers include a white granulated plastic material that fills the air spaces between the pellets. "This material behaves very much like unburned powder and will produce very conspicuous stippling of the skin around close range entry wounds."[37]

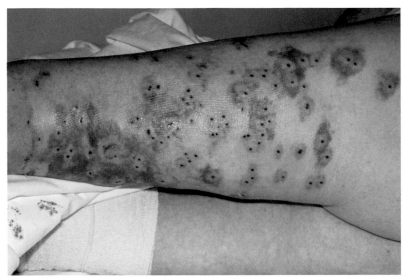

Wound patterns caused by shotgun pellets, seen here, are much different than those caused by bullets.

Exit wounds, by contrast, create their own patterns. Because of their small size, shotgun pellets rarely make exit wounds, but bullets can and do make exit wounds. For both law enforcement and medical personnel, it is essential to recognize the difference between the two, and it takes specialized training to recognize the difference between them.

Exiting the Body

Exit wounds are typically larger than entry wounds because the bullet lacerates the tissues as it forces its way up and out through the skin. The shape and size of an exit wound depends upon the size, speed, and shape of the bullet. Medical personnel may observe that blood is also present at the exit wound as well as the entrance wound, so the accurate determination of entrance and exit wound can be essential. According to Tom Warlow, retired forensic scientist with Great Britain's Forensic Science Service, in some instances the exit wounds may be "dimensionally similar to the entry wounds. In the absence of blackening or of powdering marks it is necessary to differentiate between them by checking for the presence of the abrasion ring."[38]

The size and appearance of the exit wound also depends on whether or not the bullet has become fragmented, either due to

Exit wounds, seen here, are typically larger than entry wounds because the bullet lacerates the tissues as it forces its way up and out through the skin.

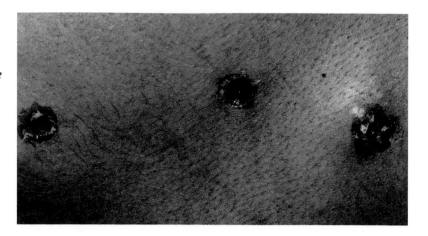

contact with an intervening object before entering the body or due to contact with bone inside the body. Fragmentation may lead to only a portion of the bullet exiting the body, with the remainder of the mass remaining in the body.

The investigation into the assassination of President Kennedy led members of the medical and law enforcement communities to push for greater research and training into the understanding of exit wounds. For example, many in the medical profession were unwilling to believe that the bullet that had exited the president's throat could have also caused Governor Connally's wounds in his chest, right arm, and thigh. However, individuals with advanced training in ballistics and wound analysis pointed to the fragmentation of the bullet; X-rays showed pieces remaining in Connally as the bullet shattered his wrist and forearm. What remained then penetrated his thigh at a shallow enough depth that two fragments of it fell out as he laid on a stretcher in the hospital.

Since that time, medical training has become more attuned to the special demands of dealing with gunshot victims. Medical examiners and investigators have come to understand the importance of accurate information about entry and exit wounds, fragmentation, and trajectories, especially when there are few or no witnesses to the shooting. One example of the advancement of the art of wound ballistics is the case of New York City resident Amadou Diallo in 1999.

A Hail of Bullets

In the early morning hours of February 4, 1999, four under-cover members of the New York Police Department were on patrol in an unmarked car in the Soundview neighborhood of the Bronx, one of the city's boroughs, in search of a serial rapist. At the same time, twenty-two-year-old Amadou Diallo, a West African immigrant, was on his way home from work. The officers stopped him outside the door to his apartment building, and, through circumstances that may never be clear, drew their weapons and shot forty-one bullets at Diallo. He was hit by nineteen of them and died at the scene. He was unarmed.

Diallo's shooting triggered a storm of protests across the city and in other locations across the United States. The officers involved said that they believed Diallo was reaching for a weapon when they opened fire, but all that was found on Diallo afterwards were his keys, a wallet, and a pager. The autopsy in this extremely sensitive case fell to Joseph Cohen of the city's Office of the Chief Medical Examiner.

Cohen's autopsy report is thorough and exacting. He documented each of the nineteen bullets that hit Diallo, noting if bullets or fragments were retrieved, the nature and dimensions of each entry and exit wound, and the path of each bullet. In addition, he carefully noted the direction each one took; for example, one wound in Diallo's left thigh was described as

> a perforating gunshot wound to the [side of the] left thigh, 35" [88.9 cm] below the top of the head. The ¼" [6.35 mm] circular/oval perforation has a 1/8" [31.8 mm] margin of abrasion. . . . There is no fouling or stippling on the adjacent skin. After perforating the skin, the bullet perforated the left thigh causing barely perceptible or no visible hemorrhage along the wound track. The exit wound is on the [middle of the front of the] left thigh, 36 ½" [92.7 cm] below the top of the head. The 5/8" [15.8 mm] oval/irregular perforation has no margin of abrasion. The direction of travel is left to right with slight back to front and barely perceptible downward deviation.[39]

Demonstators in New York City on February 26, 2000, protesting the acquittal of four New York police officers in the shooting death of Amadou Diallo.

Cohen's autopsy could have resulted in one of four conclusions. He could have found that Diallo's death was due to natural causes; that the evidence was inconclusive, leading to an "undetermined" designation; it could be ruled a suicide; or, finally, it could be ruled a homicide. He pulled no punches when it came time to list the cause of Diallo's death on his autopsy report. He ruled it a "homicide (shot by police officers)."[40] This finding, based on his ballistic wounds investigation, was a contributing factor in the Bronx district attorney's decision to charge the four officers with second-degree murder and reckless endangerment.

Ballistic Gel

Scientists use a substance called "ballistic gel" to simulate the viscosity (or thickness) and elasticity of human tissue, and how it reacts when it is impacted by a bullet or shot pellets. It is made from the same ingredients as commercial Jell-O, but lacks the colors and flavors of the dessert confection.

In the lab, a block of ballistic gel may be covered with a particular type of clothing to simulate or recreate an individual's wounds. It can be used with other materials, such as drywall, to study how a bullet may have penetrated or deflected off a wall before hitting a victim. Additionally, researchers may place a car door in front of the block to demonstrate tissue penetration of a victim inside a vehicle. Scientists also employ X-rays and high-speed photography and video to analyze the simulations.

However, ballistic gel has its limitations. According to N.C. Nicholas and J.R. Welsch of Pennsylvania State University:

> Although gelatin can simulate the density and viscosity of living human tissue, it lacks the structure of tissue. Gelatin doesn't bleed or have nerves or vessels. In addition, the human anatomy contains organs, muscle, and fat and is supported by a skeleton.

N.C. Nicholas and J.R. Welsch, *Ballistic Gelatin*. College Station, PA: Institute for Non-Lethal Defense Technologies, 2004, p. 1.

The reports generated by the medical examiner or coroner can play an important role in the investigation of a shooting. The conclusions they reach can help determine the direction of inquiries into the incident. However, some medical personnel are faced with the challenge of saving the life of a gunshot victim first before any wound analyses can begin. One such case also occurred in New York City, and also involved police officers and multiple gunshots. However, unlike Amadou Diallo, Joseph Guzman survived.

Saving a Life First, Investigating Second

Joseph Guzman, Sean Bell, and Trent Benefield were involved in an incident in the early morning hours of November 25, 2006. Undercover officers had been at the same nightclub that the three men had just left; one of the officers believed he heard Bell mention getting his weapon to settle a dispute with one of the patrons. The officers approached the men as they were sitting in Bell's vehicle. When Bell tried to flee, backing into the officers' minivan as well as backing into one of the officers twice, the police opened fire.

Bell died at the scene. Benefield and Guzman were taken to a local hospital, where trauma surgeon Albert Cooper realized Guzman was seriously wounded. He counted nineteen bullet holes. After stabilizing Guzman's breathing and blood pressure, Cooper inserted a chest tube; the amount of blood that flowed out told him that Guzman had been hit in one of his lungs. Another tube suggested more internal injuries. X-rays and a CAT scan revealed bullets and bullet damage near a kidney and to his intestines.

Subsequent surgery repaired the internal injuries. Cooper took several photos of the injuries with his cell phone, he said later, for reference in creating his incident analysis. As he had found seven bullets inside Guzman, he subtracted seven from the nineteen bullet wounds, and surmised Guzman had been shot twelve times. He later said, "Bullets either go through you,

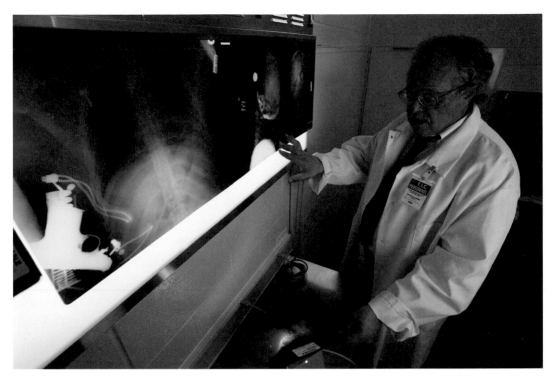

or they stay in you."[41] He deduced that the remaining twelve wounds were caused by six bullets that passed through Guzman's body. In other words, there was an entrance and an exit wound for each of the six bullets, for a total of twelve wounds.

Vincent J.M. DiMaio, former chief medical examiner in Bexar County, Texas, noted that Guzman's injuries may have been less severe because he had been inside the vehicle as the shots were fired. "If they go through metal, the bullets may have so little energy they get into the muscle or fat and then they stop,"[42] he said.

Cooper's actions represent the roles that both medical personnel and technology play in a modern shooting investigation. His advanced training, as well as his cell phone, enabled law enforcement and judicial investigators to begin to piece together an explanation of the incident. While investigators of all gunshots seek to understand the circumstances under which the weapon was fired, unfortunately, in some cases, all of the answers may never be found.

Medical personnel, using X-ray or CAT scan technologies to see inside the body, can sometimes aid forensic investigators piece together bullet evidence from shooting cases.

Unanswered Questions in Indiana

On the evening of March 4, 2008, the body of David L. Colwell, fifty-seven, of Hamilton, Ohio, was found in rural eastern Indiana, about an hour away from his home, by deputies of Franklin County's sheriff's department. Colwell was found next to his vehicle on the Fairfield Causeway, a bridge that runs across Brookville Lake, and had died of an apparent gunshot wound.

The sheriff's department enlisted the aid of the Indiana State Police, and two days later, state police sergeant John Bowling reported that state police divers had recovered a firearm from Brookville Lake near the bridge's crossing point. He told reporters, "The firearm is being sent to the Indiana State Police Laboratory for ballistic and forensic examination."[43] Colwell's body was sent to Ball Hospital in Muncie, Indiana, for an autopsy.

On March 26 Franklin County coroner Rick Gill released information surrounding Colwell's death. The report said that Colwell had died of a gunshot wound, but that the cause of death remained undetermined. At that time, Bowling of the Indiana State Police said that while foul play was not suspected, the case was still open. He declined to say if investigators felt the wound was self-inflicted. "We still don't know for sure at this point,"[44] he told the *Hamilton* (Ohio) *Journal-News*.

Colwell's death, three days before his fifty-eighth birthday, was both a tragic and unexpected event for his family. He left behind a wife, two daughters, and three grandchildren, as well as his father and a brother, and his demise leaves them with questions that perhaps may never be answered. His father, Curtis Colwell, said he could not believe that his son had committed suicide. He hopes that the investigators can help, saying, "I want to hear what they think happened."[45]

David Colwell was buried on March 8, 2008, in Hamilton. His death was still under investigation; Gill commented that the cause of death "remains undetermined until the state police finish their investigation."[46] The incident reminds both law enforcement and medical forensic investigators that science may help answer some questions in shooting incidents, but others may remain unanswered.

CHAPTER 5

Taking It to Court

The investigation of a shooting is performed on many levels, by many individuals, and with overlapping timelines. While law enforcement personnel make their first assessment of the scene, medical personnel treat the victims and begin their analyses of the wounds. While crime scene reconstructionists work at the scene, forensic scientists work in the lab to process the evidence. While the investigators begin to formulate theories, they alert the members of the local judicial system about their case. It falls to these individuals to decide if anyone is to be charged with a crime.

For these prosecutors—whether they are employed by a city, a county, a state, or the federal government—the new case may be one of hundreds they must pursue under the law. Some cases will demand a greater allocation of time and resources than others, and shooting crimes often fall into this category.

Following the discovery of a firearm in Brookville Lake beneath the bridge where David Colwell was found, state police sergeant John Bowling assured the media that testing of the firearm was going to be a high priority. However, this shifting of priorities is one example of how circumstances will change a crime lab's regular routine.

His statement meant that other tests on other cases would be delayed. However, even six weeks after Colwell's funeral, no test results had been publicized. Bowling's statement may have unintentionally reinforced a public impression that both investigators and attorneys call the "*CSI* Effect." Many in the profession believe that it has created a misleading perception in the minds of the general public about the work that crime lab personnel perform, how long it takes, and what results can be achieved.

The "CSI Effect"

On television, crime labs are portrayed as state-of-the-art, ultramodern facilities with the latest equipment and seemingly unlimited budgets. In reality, this is seldom the case. D.P. Lyle, a cardiologist and a forensic researcher, noted that unlike the crime labs depicted on popular television shows such as *CSI: Crime Scene Investigation*, real crime labs "are likely to be in windowless basements of police departments, where the norm is institutional green walls and secondhand, patchwork equipment held together with spit and chewing gum. Such are the budgets of most labs."[47]

Unlike the crime lab portrayed in *CSI*: *New York*, the New York Police Department's crime lab is not in a swanky high-rise in Manhattan. It is located in a remote part of the borough of Queens, in a sprawling office building that once housed part of the City University of New York. Although some of its equipment is state-of-the art, according to writer Jeffrey Toobin, "the seating area in the lobby includes an old minivan bench,

Real-life crime scene investigations rarely match the fast and glamourous depiction of crime scene investigations shown on fictional television programs such as CSI: New York, *seen here.*

complete with a dangling seat belt. . . . The [hair and fiber analysis] unit has two comparison microscopes, which cost fifty thousand dollars, but only one phone line, which doesn't have voicemail."[48] He quotes one supervisor as saying, "We have some of the best lab equipment in the country, maybe as good as the FBI. But for the little stuff we have to scrounge."[49]

The realities of such labs fly in the face of television portrayals, and, according to many in the field of law enforcement, investigations, and criminal justice, the fiction of television seems to have invaded the perceptions of the general public. One firearms expert recalled that when he first started in the profession:

> If you went to court and testified that two objects were fired from the same firearm, that was good enough. You used to go into court and testify about what you had seen with your naked eye. Just your word as the expert was good enough. . . . Today, the jury wants to see what we saw. Not that they would necessarily understand what we're seeing, but they know it's out there, they know it's available, and they'd like to see it, too.[50]

"There's no doubt that shows like *CSI* have affected the work," said Jim Pex, the retired chief of the Oregon State Police forensic lab in Coos Bay, Oregon, and now an independent forensic consultant. "The expectations of juries are much higher"[51] than before such shows aired, and they expect science to be able to explain much more than may actually be possible. Andrew P. Thomas, the chief prosecutor for Maricopa County, Arizona, agreed:

> On television, if the *CSI* people do their job right, the jurors will have little choice but to convict. In real life, the false expectation of plentiful scientific evidence can create a bias in the jury if this issue is not properly addressed at trial. The investigative techniques portrayed on *CSI* are not always available or even reasonable.[52]

This expectation makes the work of the attorneys and the forensic scientists all the more difficult. For the scientists, the key to meeting the challenge of the "CSI Effect" is to prepare adequately for the possibility of presenting findings in court as well as to understand the expectations of the juries.

One Investigation Leads to Another

Shortly after midnight on January 20, 2008, officers from the New York Police Department were called to Long Island College Hospital to investigate a gunshot wound. The victim had been shot in his left index finger, which, investigators later determined, had been self-inflicted.

However, while the victim was being questioned at the hospital, officers went to his apartment, where they found a pipe bomb. In the pre-dawn darkness, police started waking and evacuating the residents of his and neighboring buildings while obtaining a search warrant for the victim's apartment.

According to a report in the *New York Times*, "In all, officers found six pipe bombs, a pistol, a rifle, a shotgun, two pellet rifles, a crossbow with arrows, silencers, ammunition, a bulletproof vest and a machete." The victim was taken into custody and was charged with criminal possession of a weapon, unlawful wearing of a bulletproof vest, and reporting a false incident to police.

Subsequent interviews with the victim led police to charge the man with four counts of criminal mischief and five counts of aggravated assault in connection with a series of hate crimes in the neighborhood the previous September.

Michael Wilson, "A Man's Gunshot Wound Leads to a Weapons Trove," *New York Times*, January 21, 2008. http://www.nytimes.com/2008/01/21/nyregion/21weapons.html.

Clear and Concise

As soon as an investigation begins, law enforcement and lab personnel begin documenting their activities. Photographs, measurements, witness statements, and physical evidence such as firearms, cartridge casings, and bullets found at the scene are all carefully recorded and logged in at the responsible agency. Each investigator who handles the evidence must ensure that the chain of custody is maintained, and must be able to accurately report on each piece of evidence he or she examined.

These reports record the results of each test that lab personnel conduct. A firearms examiner details his or her study of shell casings, theorizing or determining the shell's manufacturer and caliber. A forensic scientist records the results of the gunshot residue tests from clothing and skin taken at the scene of the incident. Other lab personnel document test firings of weapons and the results of serial number restoration efforts.

For the law enforcement agency, each of these reports will include a variety of technical information based on the particular

A police officer reconstructs the path of a bullet that injured a driver. Careful analysis of the evidence is crucial when conducting a criminal investigation.

discipline. However, the forensic ballistics experts also need to ensure that the conclusions of the reports are easily decipherable by other investigators. A report that includes references to twists, lands and grooves, NIBIN, and external ballistics may be of little use to attorneys and the jury because of the scientific language and technology with which all of its readers may not be familiar.

In Minnesota, the Bureau of Criminal Apprehension has a computerized laboratory information management system with a series of templates that makes generating these reports straightforward. Forensic scientist Kurt Moline noted that when it comes time to document his findings, he opens a template that will automatically include the case number, and writes a summary of his results. Unlike a police report, which, he said, "contains every little detail about the incident, my report needs to be clear and concise. The report simply summarizes the findings."[53]

For example, a finding of exclusion from one of Moline's reports states simply:

> Comparative examinations of Item 1B (six 45 Auto caliber cartridge cases) against cartridge cases test fired in Item 1A (a Smith and Wesson Model 645 45 Auto caliber pistol bearing serial number . . .) showed the presence of different features. This means that Item 1A, in its present condition, did not fire Item 1B.[54]

The reports also serve as a reminder of previous cases that have been investigated. Consequently, if a scientist is called to testify in connection with an investigation, he or she has the concise report to refer to. However, merely having the expertise to run tests and create reports does not mean that the scientist is prepared for the unique environment of the courtroom.

Preparing for Court

The old saying that there is no substitute for experience is particularly true when dealing with a courtroom setting. The best training for dealing with the environment, before having to undergo the experience, is a combination of classroom work and simulated courtroom proceedings.

Employees of the Illinois state crime lab undergo training through a course called "Courtroom Demeanor." After the scientist has been on the job for a few months, he or she undergoes a mock trial based on one of their first cases, in order to get accustomed to speaking in a public forum. Additional mock trials include evaluations by supervisors and instructors who assess such important aspects as technical accuracy when dealing with stress.

New staff members of the Minnesota Bureau of Criminal Apprehension undergo two days of intensive training in preparing for court. Moline shared that the sessions include how to dress properly for court, public speaking, and how to address attorneys and jurors. In addition, at the conclusion of the training, the scientists are involved in a mock trial, which involves intensive interrogations. "We get grilled by other firearms examiners—the experts—who run you through worst-case scenarios to prepare you for all sorts of eventualities."[55]

Michael Haag, a firearms and toolmarks examiner for the city of Albuquerque, New Mexico, testifies in court on a regular basis. He offered some basic advice for scientists preparing to testify, whether it is the first time or the one hundredth.

> Simplify. Keeping answers basic helps all the jurors understand what you're saying, and be prepared to say, "I don't know." If you've reached a conclusion [from your analysis], be prepared to defend it, but admit it when you don't know the answer.[56]

Firearms Identification is Not Just for Humans

The U.S. Fish and Wildlife Service's (US FWS) forensics lab in Ashland, Oregon, investigates suspicious deaths in the animal kingdom. Their scientists use the same techniques on animals as their counterparts do on humans: analyzing and comparing bullets and cartridge casings, studying wound patterns, and connecting ammunition to firearms and to shooters.

In one case, officials investigated fish farmer Michael J. Zak of Massachusetts. According to the Department of Justice:

> An investigation by the FWS documented the remains of approximately 279 great blue herons, 6 ospreys, 1 bald eagle, 1 red tailed hawk, and 3 unidentified raptors, all in various states of decay along the edge of the hatchery property. Forensic examinations conducted on ten of the great blue heron carcasses collected by the FWS revealed all ten had been killed by rifle shot. . . . The FWS agents also recovered the carcass of a freshly killed immature bald eagle from the hatchery during one of their surveillances. . . . A forensic examination of the eagle determined the bird had also been shot by a high-powered rifle.

Zak was convicted in April 2007 for shooting and killing a bald eagle, a federal offense. He also pled guilty to a violation of the Migratory Bird Treaty Act related to the killing. In July, he was sentenced to six months community confinement and five years probation.

Samantha Martin, "Pair Guilty of Killing Federally Protected Birds: Bald Eagle and Hundreds of Great Blue Herons and Ospreys Killed by Owner of Trout Farm," U.S. Department of Justice, April 10, 2007. http://www.redorbit.com/news/science/898137/pair_guilty_of_killing_federally_protected_birds/index.html?source=r_science

With these skills, crime lab investigators are equipped for presenting their findings in court. Not only are they now prepared to testify about their findings, they are also prepared to assist attorneys in dealing with the "*CSI* Effect."

"Absence of Evidence Isn't Evidence of Absence"

Forensic scientist Moline has testified over one hundred times in his career, in state, local, and federal courts from North Dakota to Iowa, and, of course, in Minnesota, where he is employed. In his experience, 95 percent of his courtroom time has been at the behest of the prosecuting attorneys.

He often works with the attorney ahead of time to understand exactly what the attorney wishes him to relate. Once in the courtroom, this preparation allows him and the prosecutors to try to head off any encounters with the "*CSI* Effect" through hypothetical questions.

> They'll ask me questions like, "Why couldn't you match [a bullet to a firearm]?" or "Why couldn't you find a print on the gun?" This allows me to share what tests can be done, and what evidence might actually be there, and what isn't. . . . [Former U.S. secretary of defense Donald Rumsfeld's] phrase, "Absence of evidence isn't evidence of absence," sums it up well.[57]

Additionally, although some prosecutors want to have photographs of his work in court, he said that doing so may unwittingly detract from his evidence. In his opinion, particularly in the realm of firearms identification, using two-dimensional photographs to demonstrate what he saw in three dimensions with high-quality optics forces the jurors to be firearms and toolmarks examiners.

Michael Haag agreed. He said that in some shooting cases, the crime lab personnel may only be able to determine 5 percent of what happened. Therefore, sharing all the photographs and

Forensic scientists are often called on to testify in court cases. Whether testifying for the prosecution or the defense, the forensics expert's job is to clearly explain the evidence to the jury.

technical information gleaned from an investigation may lead the jurors to make assumptions about the other 95 percent of the incident. He painted an image of someone running across a room lit only by a strobe light while ten shots are fired. "During the time that the strobe flashes, you can tell what's going on, but what happens in between the flashes?"[58] What happens during the strobe flashes may be all the evidence the firearms examiners have for the investigation. He said, "Logic may tell you what else happened,"[59] but when testifying, the firearms examiner or forensic scientist needs to be cautious about making assumptions.

It is that process of making assumptions based on logic that separates science from speculation. Prosecutors and defense attorneys endeavor to give the whole picture about the shooting, but even when there are reliable eyewitnesses to the incident, the whole picture may be subject to interpretation. The expert testimony then moves from the realm of objectivity to that of subjectivity.

Objectivity and Subjectivity

Crime lab personnel will find themselves called to testify for both sides of cases. Moline said regardless of which side requests his presence, he points out that "the crime lab needs to be neutral"[60] when presenting testimony.

This objectivity is essential when the scientist is employed by a branch of government. The key is to ensure that the jury understands that the firearms examiner is merely presenting the lab's findings, and is making no assumptions or conclusions about the individuals involved in the case. Unfortunately, television characters talk about matching firearms to bullets or casings with 100 percent certainty. In the real world, scientists are more cautious. Hence, a firearm examiner's report will use phrases such as "showed the presence of matching features,"[61] as used by the Minnesota Bureau of Criminal Apprehension.

The need for crime lab personnel to be objective in their findings was illustrated in April 2008, when Nashville, Tennessee's, metro police department decided that its ballistics lab's work had been compromised by shortcuts taken by one examiner. According to the Nashville *Tennessean*:

> Metro shut down operation of its ballistics lab April 1 after learning from TBI [Tennessee Bureau of Investigation] that [the examiner] had incorrectly connected five bullets to the same gun. When TBI examined the evidence, it found that two of the five were fired from a gun of a different caliber, according to TBI spokeswoman Kristin Helm. "He asked the TBI not to say anything about this, and he went back and created paper work to cover up the fact that his first report was wrong," [police spokesman Don] Aaron said.[62]

While Aaron said that he was not aware of any cases in which ballistics evidence had played a major part in a conviction, the local county public defender felt that the situation called all of the lab's work into question. He said, "I think in any situation like this, the immediate assumption is that it calls into question everything the lab has ever done. That may or may not be true."[63]

23 HOURS

Time jurors spent deliberating before finding the police officers in the Diallo case not guilty.

However, other scientists are often involved in courtroom proceedings who are less constrained by the need for objectivity. These include medical personnel, such as medical examiners, coroners, and emergency services providers, as well as independent firearms examiners and forensic scientists acting as consultants. Medical personnel provide wound analyses and causes of death, and because they are not employed by a branch of the government, they are free to be as subjective as they wish with the evidence. Similarly, independent consultants, who provide services for hire to both sides, are often engaged to present subjective interpretations and to make conclusions about the evidence. This subjectivity may lead to conflicting and possibly confusing testimony for the jurors.

Conflicting Testimony

In some cases, such testimony may mean the difference between a conviction and an acquittal. One such instance involved a high-profile shooting; another involved a shooting little-known outside the city in which it occurred. Following the death of Amadou Diallo, the State of New York decided to bring charges against the four officers involved in the shooting. The case, *The People of the State of New York v. Kenneth Boss, Sean Carroll, Edward McMellon and Richard Murphy,* went to court in 2000, and featured conflicting ballistics testimony from experts on both sides.

Dr. Joseph Cohen of the New York City Office of the Chief Medical Examiner (who had performed Diallo's autopsy) testified for the prosecution, which sought to convict the officers for second-degree murder and reckless endangerment. Cohen said that, in his medical opinion, Diallo received three wounds that suggested the officers continued to fire

their weapons after Diallo was falling or had already fallen. Two struck Diallo's legs and traveled upward; Cohen said that he believed the only way that Diallo could have received these wounds as he stood upright was if one of the officers was standing directly below him and was shooting upwards. He thought that the third wound, which pierced Diallo's aorta, may have come before other shots that perforated vital internal organs because there was a lack of hemorrhaging or blood on Diallo's clothing.

The officers' defense attorneys countered with two experts who believed the evidence showed that Diallo remained standing throughout the shooting. Richard Mason, a pathologist, and Martin Fackler, a ballistics expert, both testified that they could not tell in which order the wounds were received. However, Mason felt that the sixteen wounds on Diallo's left side could have been caused as the shots hitting him began to spin him counterclockwise. He believed that the leg wounds noted by Cohen could have been received as

Four police officers charged with the shooting death of Amadou Diallo stand behind their attorney at a press conference. Conflicting ballistics testimony from experts on both sides of the case ultimately factored into the officers being found not guilty.

Diallo was falling, and both he and Fackler believed that the shot that pierced Diallo's aorta was in the last half of the hail of bullets.

The jurors deliberated approximately twenty-three hours over three days. They requested that several sections of the testimony be read back to them, including the definitions of the charges, before finding the officers not guilty of all charges on February 25, 2000. One juror said afterwards, "We were told to see the shooting from the officers' point of view, not Mr. Diallo's. The judge said to the jury they should put themselves in the shoes of the officers."[64]

"I've Been Honest Since the Beginning"

Several years later, another shooting case was concluded at the other end of the United States based in part because of forensic ballistics information. The prosecution charged the defendant with murder; the defense maintained the shooting was in self-defense.

Almost three years after the shooting in the Portland, Oregon, apartment, and more than two and a half years after being charged with his roommate Stuart Janney's murder, Karl O'Bryan entered a courtroom for a trial by judge, in which the defense waives the right to be tried by a jury. O'Bryan continued to maintain he had fired his weapon in self-defense.

The trial featured an investigation and shooting scene reconstruction by Jim Pex. Pex had been hired by O'Bryan's legal team shortly after the arrest to try to substantiate O'Bryan's claim that he had fired in self-defense. Pex studied the arrest and autopsy reports, visited the apartment, and took measurements of the scene. In his report, he made note of a distinctive feature in the apartment wall:

> Of special interest was a bullet hole in the south wall at a height of 5'10" [1.78 meters]. The bullet hole was not typical of a bullet that struck another object prior

to striking the wall. A few gunpowder particulates were visible around the hole. The angle of entry with the wall was thirty-seven degrees, which would create an intersect with the floor at 3' 9½" [1.16 meters] from the wall. . . . In order to accomplish this shot, the most probable position was sitting, kneeling or lying on the floor.[65]

This hole, along with the forensic evidence from the victim's shirt, led Pex to develop a shooting reconstruction. He theorized that the most logical way the bullet hole and Janney's wounds could have occurred was if O'Bryan was on the floor underneath Janney. He concluded:

In my opinion, the physical evidence supports his statements that he was on the floor with [Janney] above him at the time of the altercation. . . . In my opinion, [O'Bryan's] actions may be justified if he believed that his life was threatened by imminent deadly physical force against him.[66]

After the state of Oregon charged him with murder, O'Bryan was fitted with an ankle bracelet with a GPS device to track his location and movements until his trial date, which came up in February 2007. After a nine-day trial, the judge concluded that O'Bryan, now twenty-seven, had indeed acted in self-defense and found him not guilty of all charges. Afterwards, O'Bryan said, "I've been honest since the beginning."[67] He credits his exoneration to the efforts of his legal team, including an experienced investigator such as Pex, and the truth.

"Putting the Chaos of Violent Events Back in Order"

Like many retired forensic scientists, Pex now runs his own consulting business. He says he works mainly with defense teams, making his expertise available in both state and military courts. Guy Pierce also maintains a consulting business, providing crime scene and shooting incident reconstruction services as well as computer-aided graphics for courtroom use. Kurt Moline understands the continuing interest held by these retirees. "There is always something that is a bit different or interesting with almost every case."[68]

Other scientists, like Michael Haag, perform consulting and training services in addition to their full-time jobs. Haag makes it clear that to avoid conflicts of interest he cannot accept cases in Albuquerque or surrounding Bernalillo County. But, like many others in his profession, he is more than willing to spend time to share his expertise. For him, the field of firearms identification and forensic ballistics is both fascinating and rewarding.

People who work in the field of forensics require many hours of training not only inside a lab, but out in the field as well. Here, a staged crime scene acts as a training tool for these officers.

There is a lot of satisfaction in putting the chaos of violent events back in order. . . . When you have that one piece (or perhaps a lot of pieces) come together to give particular clarity to a violent event, it is quite rewarding. There is some "thrill of the hunt" aspect, but it isn't relating to hunting a person. It relates to hunting for evidence, or hunting the meaning of that evidence.[69]

Notes

Introduction:
The "D.C. Snipers"

1. "Shooting Victims," *Gazette.net*, October 15, 2002. http://www.gazette.net/gazette_archive/2002/200241/montgomerycty/county/124963-1.html.

2. Quoted in Jeanne Meserve, Kelli Arena, Gary Tuchman, and Barbara Starr, "Ballistics Match Rifle to Sniper Attacks," *CNN.com*, October 25, 2002. http://archives.cnn.com/2002/US/South/10/24/sniper.shootings/.

Chapter 1:
Firearms and Bullets

3. N.E. Genge, *The Forensic Casebook: The Science of Crime Investigation*. New York: Ballantine Books, 2002, p. 104.

4. David Owen, *Hidden Evidence: Forty True Crimes and How Forensic Science Helped Solve Them*. Buffalo NY: Firefly Books, 2000, p. 17.

5. Keith Skinner, Martin Fido, and Alan Moss, "The Development of Ballistics," November 30, 2006. http://www.historybytheyard.co.uk/pc_gutteridge.htm.

6. Quoted in Keith Inman and Norah Rudin, *Principles and Practice of Criminalistics: The Profession of Forensic Science*. Boca Raton, FL: CRC Press, 2001, p. 37.

7. Katherine Ramsland, "The Pressure is On," *Criminal Mind: Forensics & Investigation*, 2007. http://www.care2.com/c2c/groups/disc.html?gpp=5154&pst=843990.

8. Inman and Rudin, p. 37.

9. Ramsland, "The Pressure is On."

Chapter 2: Evidence
Left Behind

10. Sari Horwitz and Michael E. Ruane, *Sniper: Inside the Hunt for the Killers Who Terrorized the Nation*. New York: Random House, 2003, p. 119.

11. "SWGGUN Admissibility Resource Kit," *Swggun.org*, November 29, 2007. http://www.swggun.org/resources/resourcekit.htm.

12. Sally A. Schehl, "Firearms and Toolmarks in the FBI Laboratory, Part 1," *Forensic Science Communications*, April 2000. http://www.fbi.gov/hq/lab/fsc/backissu/april2000/schehl1.htm.

13. "SWGGUN Admissibility Resource Kit."

14. Telephone interview with Kurt Moline, April 1, 2008.

15. Charles A. Moose and Charles Fleming, *Three Weeks in October: The Manhunt for the Serial Sniper*. New York: Dutton, 2003, pp. 275–76.

16. Moose and Fleming, p. 275.

17. Moline, April 1, 2008.

18. Schehl, "Firearms and Toolmarks in the FBI Laboratory, Part 1."

19. Moline, April 1, 2008.

20. Moline, April 1, 2008.

21. Moline, April 1, 2008.

22. Edward C. Klatt, "Examination of Gunshot Residue," The Internet Pathology Laboratory for Medical Education, University of Utah, 2008. http://library.med.utah.edu/WebPath/TUTORIAL/GUNS/GUNGSR.html.

23. Moline, April 1, 2008.

Chapter 3: The Flight of a Bullet

24. Telephone interview with Guy Pierce, April 7, 2008.

25. Pierce, April 7, 2008.

26. Quoted in "The Case for the Prosecution," *Wichita Eagle*, April 3, 2008. http://videos.kansas.com/vmix_hosted_apps/p/media?id=1803797&item_index=22&genre_id=3020&sort=NULL.

27. Pierce, April 7, 2008.

28. Pierce, April 7, 2008.

29. Personal correspondence with Ron Sylvester, April 10, 2008.

30. Pierce, April 7, 2008.

31. Pierce, April 7, 2008.

32. Paul Thomas, "Shooting Victim: 'Scarf Saved My Life,'" March 26, 2008. http://www.wkyc.com/news/local/news_article.aspx?storyid=85784&catid=64.

33. Quoted in Thomas, "Shooting Victim: 'Scarf Saved My Life.'"

34. Office of the Inspector General, "A Review of the September 2005 Shooting Incident Involving the Federal Bureau of Investigation and Filiberto Ojeda Ríos: Chapter Four: Findings of the Puerto Rico Institute of Forensic Sciences," usdoj.gov, August 2006. http://www.usdoj.gov/oig/special/s0608/chapter4.htm#IV.

Chapter 4: After the Impact

35. Edward C. Klatt, "Criminalistics Laboratory Methods: Surgical Pathology Description of Bullets," The Internet Pathology Laboratory for Medical Education, University of Utah, 2008. http://library.med.utah.edu/WebPath/TUTORIAL/GUNS/GUNLAB.html.

36. Lucien C. Haag, *Shooting Incident Reconstruction*. Burlington, MA: Academic Press, 2006, p. 235.

37. Lucien Haag, p. 242.

38. Tom Warlow, *Firearms, the Law, and Forensic Ballistics, 2nd ed.* Boca Raton, FL: CRC Press, 2005, p. 243.

39. Joseph Cohen, "Report of Autopsy, Case No. Bx99O0498," *CourtTV.com*, May 24, 2002. http://www.courttv.com/archive/national/diallo/autopsy.html.

40. Cohen, "Report of Autopsy, Case No. Bx99O0498."

41. Quoted in Michael Wilson, "On Stand in Officers' Trial, Surgeon Details Injuries to Passenger in Sean Bell's Car," *New York Times*, April 3, 2008. http://www.nytimes.com/2008/04/03/ nyregion/03bell.html?_r=1&sq=On% 20Stand%20in%20Officers'%20Trial,% 20Surgeon%20Details%20Injuries%20 to%20Passenger%20in%20Sean%20Bell 's%20Car&st=cse&adxnnl=1&scp=1&a dxnnlx=1219334746-o2BHdGfnEPYvr iMIsX887w&oref=slogin.

42. Quoted in John Eligon, "One Bullet Can Kill, but Sometimes 20 Don't, Survivors Show," *New York Times*, April 3, 2008. http://www.nytimes.com/2008/04/03/ nyregion/03shot.html?scp=1&sq=One %20Bullet%20Can%20Kill,%20but% 20Sometimes%2020%20Don%92t,%20 Survivors%20Show&st=cse.

43. Quoted in "Police: Body Found on Fairfield Causeway Had Gunshot Wound," *Palladium-Item* (Richmond, IN), March 7, 2008. http://www.topix. com/city/brookville-in/2008/03/police- body-found-on-fairfield-causeway-had- gunshot-wound.

44. Quoted in Lauren Pack, "Police Don't Suspect Foul Play in Shooting Death," *Hamilton Journal News*, March 27, 2008. http://www.swocol.com/search/content/ oh/story/news/local/2008/03/26/hjn- 032708colwell.html.

45. Quoted in Pack, "Police Don't Suspect Foul Play in Shooting Death."

46. Telephone interview with Rick Gill, April 18, 2008.

Chapter 5: Taking It to Court

47. D.P. Lyle, *Forensics for Dummies*. Indianapolis: Wiley Publishing, 2004, p. 328.

48. Jeffrey Toobin, "The CSI Effect: The Truth About Forensic Science," *New Yorker*, May 7, 2007. http://www. newyorker.com/reporting/2007/05/07/ 070507fa_fact_toobin?currentPage=all.

49. Quoted in Toobin, "The CSI Effect: The Truth About Forensic Science."

50. Quoted in Connie Fletcher, *Every Contact Leaves a Trace: Crime Scene Experts Talk About Their Work from Discovery Through Verdict*. New York: St. Martin's Press, 2006, pp. 339–40.

51. Telephone interview with Jim Pex, April 14, 2008.

52. Andrew P. Thomas, "The CSI Effect: Fact or Fiction," *The Yale Law Journal*, February 1, 2006. http://www.the pocketpart.org/2006/02/thomas.html.

53. Telephone interview with Kurt Moline, April 23, 2008.

54. Personal correspondence with Kurt Moline, April 23, 2008.

55. Moline, telephone interview, April 23, 2008.

56. Telephone interview with Michael Haag, April 21, 2008.

57. Moline, telephone interview, April 23, 2008.

58. Telephone interview with Michael Haag, April 20, 2008.

59. Michael Haag, April 20, 2008.

60. Moline, telephone interview, April 23, 2008.

61. Moline, personal correspondence, April 23, 2008.

62. Quoted in Kate Howard, "Ballistics Lab Shut Because of Errors: Outcome of Metro Cases May Be Called into Doubt," *Tennessean*, April 12, 2008. http://m.tennessean.com/news.jsp?key=67153.

63. Quoted in Howard, "Ballistics Lab Shut Because of Errors: Outcome of Metro Cases May Be Called into Doubt."

64. Quoted in Bryan Robinson, "Diallo Jurors Say They Had No Choice But to Acquit," *CourtTV.com*, February 28, 2000. http://www.courttv.com/archive/national/diallo/022800_aftermath_ctv.html.

65. Jim Pex, Shooting reconstruction report, amended January 31, 2007.

66. Pex, January 31, 2007.

67. Quoted in Aimee Green, "Judge Frees Man in Friend's Killing," *Oregonian*, February 21, 2007.

68. Personal correspondence with Kurt Moline, April 29, 2008.

69. Michael Haag, April 20, 2008.

Glossary

ballistic gel: A gelatin that is used to simulate living tissue for firearms and forensic testing analysis.

ballistics: The science of projectiles in motion.

breechface: The area at the rear of the cartridge chamber against which a shell is placed at loading and firing.

bullet: A small metal projectile, part of a cartridge, for firing from firearms.

caliber: For firearms, caliber is the approximate diameter of the circle formed by the tops of the lands of a rifled barrel. For ammunition, caliber is a numerical term included in a cartridge name to indicate the nominal bullet diameter.

cartridge: A single unit of ammunition consisting of the casing, primer, and propellant with one or more projectile(s).

casing: The container for all the other components that comprise a cartridge.

chain of custody: The documentation that records the disposition of evidence from and materials related to an investigation.

clip: A separate cartridge container to rapidly reload the magazine of a firearm. According to the Association for Firearm and Tool Mark Examiners, this term is sometimes improperly used to describe removable magazines.

exterior ballistics: The branch of applied mechanics that studies the motion of a projectile from the muzzle of a firearm to the target.

Firearms Identification: A discipline of forensic science that seeks to determine if a bullet, cartridge case, or other ammunition component was fired by a particular firearm.

full metal jacket: A projectile in which the bullet jacket encloses the entire bullet, with the usual exception of the base.

grooves: Spiral-shaped channels cut into the bore of a firearm barrel to give a projectile its spinning motion.

gun shot residue (GSR): Residue from the combustion of gunpowder and primer during weapons fire.

IBIS: Short for Integrated Ballistics Identification System. A computer program that assists firearms identification technicians to compare new cartridge casings and/or bullets to samples previously entered into the system.

interior ballistics: The branch of ballistics dealing with all aspects of combustion occurring within a firearm, including pressure development and motion of the projectile along the barrel of the weapon.

land: The raised portion between the grooves in a rifled bore.

lever action: A design in which the breech mechanism is cycled by an external lever.

long gun: Any firearm fitted with a stock and designed to be used while held with both hands and supported by a shoulder.

magazine: In firearms, a container for cartridges that has a spring and follower to feed those cartridges into the chamber of a firearm. The magazine may be detachable or an integral part of the firearm.

NIBIN: Short for National Integrated Ballistics Information Network. Maintained by the Bureau of Alcohol, Tobacco, Firearms and Explosives, this national network produces correlations between submitted images of casings and/or bullets and potential regional or national matches.

pump action: An action that features a movable forearm which is manually set in motion parallel to the barrel by the shooter.

round: A military term for a cartridge.

semi-jacketed: A projectile with a partial jacket, exposing a lead nose.

striations: Contour variations, generally microscopic, on the surface of an object caused by a combination of force and motion.

terminal ballistics: The branch of ballistics that deals with the effects of a projectile's impact on the target.

toolmarks: Any number of impressions left on softer material by use of an object of a harder material. In firearms identification, toolmarks are any number of impressions left on weapons and ammunition, including during loading, discharge, and ejection.

trajectory: The path of a projectile from muzzle to target.

wound ballistics: A subset of terminal ballistics dealing with the behavior of projectiles in tissue and tissue simulations. It includes studies of bullet velocity, expansion, fragmentation, and deformation, penetration characteristics, and velocity loss due to the perforation of tissue and tissue simulations.

For More Information

Books

Susan Echaore-McDavid, *Career Opportunities in Law Enforcement, Security and Protective Services*. New York: Checkmark Books, 2006. Working with professionals in the various fields, the author relates how to work towards a career in dozens of specialties, from park ranger to medical examiner, as well as earnings potential and career advancement.

Colin Evans, *The Casebook of Forensic Detection: How Science Solved 100 of the World's Most Baffling Cases*. New York: Berkeley Trade, 2007. Examines a variety of famous and little-known cases, including the Sacco and Vanzetti case. Cases are organized by the forensic techniques used in each investigation.

N.E. Genge, *The Forensic Casebook: The Science of Crime Scene Investigation*. New York: Ballantine Books, 2002. Concise information about a variety of techniques used in crime scene investigations, with fascinating anecdotes from professionals in the field.

John Houde, *Crime Lab: A Guide for Nonscientists*. Ventura, CA: Calico Press, 1999. Written in a conversational style, this book takes the reader through a variety of scientific techniques used in investigations.

D.P. Lyle, *Forensics for Dummies*. Indianapolis: Wiley Publishing, 2004. A comprehensive and entertaining guide to forensic science.

Joe Nickell and John F. Fischer, *Crime Science: Methods of Forensic Detection*. Lexington: University Press of Kentucky, 1998. Nickell and Fischer, nationally-recognized forensic scientists, share step-by-step descriptions of crime scene investigations.

David Owen, *Hidden Evidence: Forty True Crimes and How Forensic Science Helped Solve Them*. Buffalo, NY: Firefly Books, 2000. Richly illustrated, this book gives behind-the-scenes looks at some famous cases.

Richard Platt, *Crime Scene: The Ultimate Guide to Forensic Science*. New York: DK Adult, 2006. An introduction to the world of forensic sciences and criminal investigations, with insights into techniques used.

Larry Ragle, *Crime Scene*. New York: Avon Books, 2002. Written by a California forensic scientist, this book examines his most memorable cases over a forty-year career.

Katherine Ramsland, *The C.S.I. Effect*. New York: Berkley Boulevard Books, 2006. The author uses plot lines from the popular television episodes to connect to real-life events, and to point out where fact leaves off and fiction begins.

Katherine Ramsland, *The Forensic Science of C.S.I.* New York: Berkeley Trade, 2001. Detailed accounts of the techniques used in crime scene investigations, with interviews with leading members of the field.

Reports

Office of the Inspector General of the United States, "A Review of the September 2005 Shooting Incident Involving the Federal Bureau of Investigation and Filiberto Ojeda Ríos," August 2006. A comprehensive but fascinating account of the events surrounding the Ojeda incident. The narrative includes photographs of the site and detailed recollections of the agents involved.

Periodicals

Sally A. Schehl, "Firearms and Toolmarks in the FBI Laboratory, Part 1," *Forensic Science Communications*, April 2000. An excellent introduction to the science of firearms and toolmarks identification.

Ron Sylvester, "ID Key as Murder Trial Opens," *Wichita Eagle*, April 3, 2008, page 6B. First in a series of articles about the shooting of Xavier Worley and death of Laquishia Starr.

Andrew P. Thomas, *The* CSI *Effect: Fact or Fiction*, 115 Yale L.J. Pocket Part 70, 2006. The author examines the premise that television programs such as *CSI: Crime Scene Investigation* affect real-life criminal proceedings.

Jeffrey Toobin, "The CSI Effect: The Truth About Forensic Science," *The New Yorker*, May 7, 2007. Behind the scenes at the real-life New York City Police Department crime lab.

Michael Wilson, "On Stand in Officers' Trial, Surgeon Details Injuries to Passenger in Sean Bell's Car," *New York Times*, April 3, 2008. Detailed account of advanced forensic wound analysis in Joseph Guzman's shooting.

Internet Sources

Gazette.net, "Shooting Victims," October 15, 2002. http://www.gazette.net/gazette_archive/2002/200241/montgomerycty/county/124963-1.html#3. Biographical sketches of the victims of the "D.C. Snipers."

Jeanne Meserve, Kelli Arena, Gary Tuchman, and Barbara Starr, "Ballistics Match Rifle to Sniper Attacks," *CNN.com*, October 25, 2002. http://archives.cnn.com/2002/US/South/10/24/sniper.shootings/. Coverage of the arrest of John Muhammad and Lee Boyd Malvo.

Palladium-Item (Richmond, IN), "Police: Body Found on Fairfield Causeway Had Gunshot Wound," March 7, 2008. http://www.topix.com/city/brookville-in/2008/03/police-body-found-on-fairfield-causeway-had-gunshot-wound. First of several articles documenting the investigation into the gunshot death of David L. Colwell.

Web Sites

Association of Firearm and Tool Mark Examiners (http://www.afte.org/index. htm). Dedicated to the advancement of firearm and tool mark examinations, this site includes a variety of resources as well as forums for examiners and resources for advanced training.

Basic Equipment for Crime Scene Investigators (www.feinc.net/equipmt. htm). Compiled by a retired master sergeant with the Illinois State Police, who now runs a consulting business. A fascinating look at the requirements for the well-equipped CSI in the field, with photographs.

Crime-Scene-Investigator.net's "Becoming a Crime Scene Investigator" (www.crime-scene-investigator.net) has step-by-step information and advice on considering a career as a CSI.

The Federal Bureau of Investigation (FBI)'s Kids Page (www.fbi.gov/fbikids.htm) offers grade-specific activities and stories about FBI investigations, and the techniques used to analyze the evidence.

FirearmsID.com (www.firearmsid.com). Maintained by a retired forensic scientist, this site covers a wide variety of techniques and history of forensic firearms identification. Also includes exercises and interactive demonstrations (free registration required for some pages).

Forensic Magazine's "Who Says You Can't Do That" series looks at becoming a CSI (www.forensicmag.com/articles. asp?pid=164). Written by a crime scene consultant and trainer, this article offers excellent advice and alternatives for those interested in CSI careers.

How Stuff Works, "How Crime Scene Investigation Works" (http://science. howstuffworks.com/csi.htm). Written with the assistance of a member of the Colorado Bureau of Investigation, this multipart series takes the reader through recognizing, gathering, and analyzing evidence.

International Association for Identification (theiai.org). This organization includes members from a variety of forensic science disciplines, including firearms identification. The site also includes excellent links to forensic identification guides plus an RSS feed for job announcements.

Index

Picture Credits

About the Author

Andrew A. Kling worked as a National Park Service ranger in locations across the United States for over fifteen years. He now works as a writer and editor for a variety of nonprofit organizations, and as an interpretive media developer and consultant. He enjoys hockey, technology, vexillology, and spending time with his wife and their famous Norwegian Forest cat, Chester.

The author wishes to thank Kay Jackson, upon whose foundation this book was built; Michael Haag, Chuck Harris, Kurt Moline, Lt. Jim Pex, and Sgt. Guy Pierce for their valuable time as well as their helpful suggestions and direction during this project; and my wife, who has learned to tolerate my early morning ramblings of seemingly disconnected inspirations.